BROADMAN COMMENTS JUNE-AUG. '98

13 Ready-To-Teach Bible Study Lessons

Broadman Comments June-Aug. '98

13 Ready-To-Teach Bible Study Lessons

Robert J. Dean
William E. Anderson
James E. Taulman

Based on the International Sunday School Lessons

Each Plan Includes These Sections: Studying the Bible · Applying the Bible · Teaching the Bible

Nashville, Tennessee

4217–54
ISBN: 0–8054–1754–0

Dewey Decimal Classification: 268.61
Subject Heading: SUNDAY SCHOOL LESSONS—COMMENTARIES

Broadman Comments *is published quarterly by Broadman & Holman Publishers, 127 Ninth Avenue, North, Nashville, Tennessee 37234*

When ordered with other church literature, it sells for $5.99 per quarter. Second class postage paid at Nashville, Tennessee

ISSN: 0068–2721

POSTMASTER: Send address change to *Broadman Comments,* Customer Service Center, 127 Ninth Avenue, North
Nashville, Tennessee 37234

Library of Congress Catalog Card Number: 45–437
Printed in the United States of America

WRITERS

STUDYING THE BIBLE

Robert J. Dean continues the theological traditions of *Broadman Comments* while adding his own fresh insights. Dean is retired from the Baptist Sunday School Board and is a Th.D. graduate of New Orleans Seminary

APPLYING THE BIBLE

William E. Anderson has been pastor of Calvary Baptist Church, Clearwater, Florida, since 1975. Calvary's weekly services are telecast on various local stations and by satellite over Christian Network, Inc., on the Dish Network.

TEACHING THE BIBLE

James E. Taulman is a freelance writer in Nashville, Tennessee. Prior to that, Taulman was an editor of adult Sunday school materials for the Baptist Sunday School Board.

ABBREVIATIONS AND TRANSLATIONS

Scripture passages are from the authorized King James Version of the Bible. Other translations used:

GNB. From the Good News Bible, the Bible in Today's English Version, Old Testament © American Bible Society 1976, New Testament © American Bible Society 1966, 1971, 1976; used by permission.

NASB. From the New American Standard Bible. © The Lockman Foundation, 1960, 1962, 1963, 1968, 1971, 1972, 1973, 1975, 1977. Used by Permission.

NEB. From the New English Bible, © the Delegates of the Oxford University Press and the Syndics of the Cambridge University Press, 1961, 1970; reprinted by permission.

NIV. From the Holy Bible, New International Version. Copyright © 1973, 1978, 1984 by International Bible Society. Used by permission.

RSV. From The Revised English Bible. Copyright © Oxford University Press and Cambridge University Press, 1989. Reprinted by permission.

NRSV. From the New Revised Standard Version of the Bible, copyright © 1989 by the Division of Christian Education of the National Council of Churches of Christ in the United States of America. Used by permission. All rights reserved.

Contents

Wisdom for Living

June

July

August

Wisdom for Living (Ecclesiastes, Job, Proverbs)

JUNE
JULY
AUGUST
1998

INTRODUCTION

This quarter's studies are based on passages from three of the Wisdom Books of the Old Testament. Ecclesiastes probes questions about how to find meaning in life. Job struggles with finding an answer to why righteous people suffer. Proverbs provides practical wisdom for everyday living.

Unit I, "When Human Wisdom Fails," consists of four lessons that deal with difficult questions raised in Ecclesiastes and Job. The first lesson deals with the search for meaning in the Book of Ecclesiastes. The second lesson sets forth questions asked by God, Satan, and Job. The third lesson deals with the attempt of Job's three friends to answer Job's questions and Job's dissatisfaction with their answers. Lesson 4 focuses on Job's responses to God's questions.

Unit II, "Proverbs on Living a Disciplined Life," consists of four lessons from Proverbs on how a wise person should live. Lesson 1 identifies the blessings of listening to wisdom. Lesson 2 shows how wisdom is expressed by trust in God. Lesson 3 presents practical advice about how to be a good neighbor. The final lesson in the unit contrasts how wise and foolish people respond to God's law.

Unit III, "Two Ways—The Way of Wisdom and the Way of Foolishness," contrasts two ways of life. The first lesson shows that the way of wisdom leads to happiness and the way of foolishness leads to destruction. Lesson 2 deals with proverbs about the blessing of work and the sin of laziness. Lesson 3 contrasts helpful and harmful words. Lesson 4 emphasizes the importance of being slow to get angry. Lesson 5 provides some guidelines for family relationships.

Books of Poetry

The Bible's many literary forms fall into two broad categories: prose and poetry. Prose includes laws, historical narratives, letters, and normal dialogue and teachings. Poetry includes poems, songs, proverbs, drama, and prophecy.

Many English translations print poetry with each line (not each verse or each paragraph) beginning on a new line.

The Books of Job, Psalms, Proverbs, Ecclesiastes, Song of Solomon are called Books of Poetry. All or most of these five books are in poetic form. For example, the only prose sections of Job are the prologue, the epilogue, and the brief introductions to the speeches.

Not all Bible poetry is in these five books. Much of the prophets is poetry, and songs and proverbs are scattered throughout other Bible books.

More Questions than Answers

JUNE 7 1998

Basic Passages: Ecclesiastes 1:1–3; 2:1–4, 10–15; 4:1–3; 12:1, 13–14

Focal Passages: Ecclesiastes 1:1–3; 2:1–2, 10–13; 4:1–3; 12:1, 13–14

The three Bible books traditionally assigned to Solomon are Proverbs, Ecclesiastes, and Song of Solomon. These are among the Wisdom Books of the Old Testament, but each is distinctive not only from one another but also from other Bible books. In fact, when decisions were made about which books to include in the Holy Scriptures, the last two of these aroused considerable debate. Yet each makes a unique contribution to the message of the Bible. Song of Solomon exalts married love. Ecclesiastes shows the importance of finding meaning in life.

Study Aim: *To identify the ways in which the author sought meaning in life and his conclusions about each way*

STUDYING THE BIBLE

OUTLINE AND SUMMARY

I. Does Life Have Meaning? (Eccles. 1:1–3)

1. The Preacher (1:1)

2. His theme (1:2)

3. His question (1:3)

II. Search for Meaning (Eccles. 2:1–4, 10–15; 4:1–3)

1. Pleasure (2:1–3)

2. Possessions (2:4, 10–11)

3. Wisdom (2:12–15)

4. Justice (4:1–3)

III. Conclusions (Eccles. 12:1, 13–14)

1. Remember the Creator in youth (12:1)

2. Fear and obey God (12:13–14)

The author introduced himself as the Preacher, king in Jerusalem (1:1). His theme was the emptiness of life (1:2). He questioned the value of a lifetime of work (1:3). He sought satisfaction in pleasure, but found it empty (2:1–3). He sought meaning in possessions, yet he found no lasting satisfaction (2:4, 10–11). He decided wisdom was better than folly, but that death comes to both the wise and the foolish (2:12–15). Finding oppression in society, he said that it was better to be dead or never to have been born (4:1–3). The Preacher called the young to remember the Creator (12:1). He stated humanity's duty to fear and obey God (12:13–14).

I. Does Life Have Meaning? (Eccles. 1:1–3)

1. The Preacher (1:1)

1 The words of the Preacher, the son of David, king in Jerusalem.

The word translated "Preacher" referred to the person who assembled the congregation in order to speak to them. Thus it is usually translated either as "Preacher" or "Teacher."

The author uses this title rather than his name, although the last part of verse 1 was intended to identify Solomon (see also 1:12). The author did not write this book as royal decrees but spoke as a preacher or teacher, using Solomon's personal quest for meaning as the basis for what he preached and taught to others.

2. His theme (1:2)

2 Vanity of vanities, saith the Preacher, vanity of vanities; all is vanity.

The word "vanity" appears repeatedly in Ecclesiastes. The Hebrew word means "vapor" or "breath." One use of the word stresses the shortness and uncertainty of human life (see Ps. 144:4; James 4:14). The word also has the idea of "emptiness." A vapor lacks substance. In several verses (see 1:14; 2:11), the word is described as "vexation of spirit." Since the Hebrew word for "spirit" can also mean "breath" or "wind," this phrase is often translated "chasing after wind." This suggests not only the idea of being empty but also the idea of being "meaningless" or "absurd." You can never catch the wind; and if you did, you would have nothing anyway.

3. His question (1:3)

3 What profit hath a man of all the labour which he taketh under the sun?

Another way to word the question is this: When our lives come to an end, what will we have to show for a lifetime of work? This was the central question that the author set out to answer. Since his quest was completed before he wrote, he stated in verse 2 his answer to the question in verse 3. His answer was that we have nothing to show for a lifetime of work because life is not only short and uncertain but also empty and meaningless.

II. Search for Meaning (Eccles. 2:1–4,10–14; 4:1–3)

1. Pleasure (2:1–3)

1 I said in mine heart, Go to now, I will prove thee with mirth, therefore enjoy pleasure: and, behold, this also is vanity.

2 I said of laughter, It is mad: and of mirth, What doeth it?

Much of Ecclesiastes is the Preacher's description of his search for an answer to his question in 1:3. He set out to test or examine various ways in which people search for meaning for their lives. Pleasure was one of the ways he tested. The word translated "pleasure" in verse 1 means "good." He set out to discover if enjoying a good time gives meaning to life. He employed "mirth" (enjoyment), laughter, and wine (2:3). His conclusion was that this way of seeking meaning is only "vanity" or "vapor." The question at the end of verse 2 refers back to the question in 1:3. In other words, he did not find lasting profit in seeking a good time. (See also Prov. 14:13.)

2. Possessions (2:4, 10–11)

> **10 And whatsoever mine eyes desired I kept not from them, I withheld not my heart from any joy; for my heart rejoiced in all my labour: and this was my portion of all my labour.**
>
> **11 Then I looked on all the works that my hands had wrought, and on the labour that I had laboured to do: and, behold, all was vanity and vexation of spirit, and there was no profit under the sun.**

Verse 4 introduces a new part of the Preacher's quest for meaning. He sought it in building houses and planting vineyards. Possessions are not an end in themselves, but they pave the way to the so-called "good life" that is supposed to come with enough money and possessions.

Verse 10 describes how completely he threw himself into seeking lasting satisfaction in possessions. He went after whatever he wanted. The last part of verse 10 testifies that he found for a time some pleasure and some profit in this way of life. However, verse 11 states his final conclusion. In retrospect, he pronounced his selfish quest for possessions as futile.

This is always the end of a purely selfish quest. Notice in verses 10–11 and other verses how often appear the words "I," "my," "mine," "myself." Does this remind you of Jesus' story in Luke 12:16–21? The same words predominate. The man assumed that he could find satisfaction for himself in his work, his possessions, his wealth, and his retirement. God called that man a fool.

3. Wisdom (2:12–15)

> **12 And I turned myself to behold wisdom, and madness, and folly: for what can the man do that cometh after the king? even that which hath been already done.**
>
> **13 Then I saw that wisdom excelleth folly, as far as light excelleth darkness.**

Having failed to find ultimate satisfaction in either pleasure or possessions, the teacher devoted all his energies to consider wisdom and knowledge. We would probably say that he staked his hope on education and common sense. Verse 13 states his initial judgment. He concluded that wisdom was much better than foolishness and ignorance. It was like the difference between light and darkness.

However, the last part of verse 12 and verses 14–15 render a more sober judgment on wisdom as a final solution. The reality of death forced itself upon the wise man. He realized that wise men as well as fools must die, and he concluded that in the long run the wise man is really no better than the fool since both must die.

The last part of verse 12 poses problems for translators. Some translators assume Solomon was thinking of his successor, recognizing that his son could not inherit whatever wisdom his father had attained. Other translators assume that the point is more general, although the result is about the same. Does history show that human beings have grown more wise with the passing of generations? We have improved technology, but we have not solved any of the basic human problems that have afflicted humans since the Garden of Eden.

4. Justice (4:1–3)

1 So I returned, and considered all the oppressions that are done under the sun: and behold the tears of such as were oppressed, and they had no comforter; and on the side of the oppressors there was power; but they had no comforter.

2 Wherefore I praised the dead which are already dead more than the living which are yet alive.

3 Yea, better is he than both they, which hath not yet been, who hath not seen the evil work that is done under the sun.

The Preacher turned from his personal quest for meaning and looked at society as a whole. Perhaps he could find meaning by looking at this larger picture. He saw a world of oppression. The oppressors had all the power, and they used it to exploit those without power. The oppressed had only their tears; but no one could offer them comfort, which would be possible only if they would receive justice. The Preacher saw no justice in the social, economic, or political life of his day. He had been looking for profit or value of living; instead of finding value, he found evil and oppression.

Verses 2–3 deliver the Preacher's bleak conclusion about trying to find meaning in justice. Nothing he wrote better states the futility of life or the dead-end despair about life. Verse 2 says that the dead are better off than the living, since the living must live in such an unjust world. Verse 3 says that people who have never been born are better off than either the living or the dead.

III. Conclusions (Eccles. 12:1, 13–14)

1. Remember the Creator in youth (12:1)

1 Remember now thy Creator in the days of thy youth, while the evil days come not, nor the years draw nigh, when thou shalt say, I have no pleasure in them;

This famous verse is part of a larger passage dealing with making the most of life in youth and in old age. The young are advised to enjoy life (11:7–10). Ecclesiastes 12:1 is a transition verse that ties together youth and old age. Verses 2–7 describe in figurative language the aging process, including its negative aspects. Verse 1 exhorts the young to remember the Creator while they are still young and have all of life before them. Youth seldom recognize how short and uncertain life is. The Preacher, writing as a wise old man, pleaded with youth to honor and obey the Creator while they had the opportunity.

2. Fear and obey God (12:13–14)

13 Let us hear the conclusion of the whole matter: Fear God, and keep his commandments: for this is the whole duty of man.

14 For God shall bring every work into judgment, with every secret thing, whether it be good, or whether it be evil.

After the mood of despair that pervades most of the book, we are taken by surprise by this conclusion. In fact, some Bible scholars wonder if the Preacher wrote these words. They theorize that a later editor may have added a more traditional ending to the book. On the other hand, could not the rest of the book be background for this positive counterpoint? The bulk of the book shows how futile life is without God. Thus, people ought to fear and obey God.

This was obviously a great leap of faith for the person who wrote the rest of the book. Most of his questions were either still unanswered or he had found unsatisfying answers for them. His search for meaning had led him nowhere. His search for justice had produced even more despair. He could have concluded that all of this meant that either God does not exist or He is unconcerned with the plight of humanity. Instead, at the end, he concluded that youth should remember the Creator and that everyone should fear and obey God. He even affirmed that God would eventually judge good and evil. He still did not understand God or God's ways, but he chose reverence and obedience as the best response to make.

APPLYING THE BIBLE

1. True philosophy. Along with the Book of Job, Ecclesiastes is commonly considered to be one of the two most philosophical of all the books of the Bible. Philosophy asks, essentially, "What is the true meaning of life?" Although the Preacher might never have thought of denying God, he came to a common conclusion with Francis Bacon: "A little philosophy inclineth man's mind to atheism, but depth of philosophy bringeth men's minds about to religion." If philosophy is the love of wisdom (which is what the word *philosophy* literally means), then there can be no conflict between philosophy and God's wisdom or truth.

2. Popular philosophy. One of the benefits of considering philosophical matters is that it forces us to clarify what we believe about essential matters. Socrates put it like this: "The unexamined life is not worth living." All of us are philosophers whether we know it or not. During one of my early pastorates, I asked a farmer about eternal things. "Well, he said, "I guess life's mostly just eatin' and sleepin'." He did not know that he was espousing, in that statement, the core belief of an ancient philosophy called Epicureanism.

3. The meaning of life. The three overriding questions of human existence are:

- Where did I come from?
- What does life mean?
- What happens after life on earth?

The Book of Ecclesiastes references all three, but focuses on the second one.

4. God's three roles. A biblical worldview has, essentially, three components:

- God is Creator,

- God is Caregiver (Sustainer or Provider), and
- God is Consummator.

The author of Ecclesiastes emphasizes all three of the divine roles. He sees God as Creator (12:11), Caregiver (1:4–7, 5:9, 18–20), and as Consummator (12:7, 14).

5. Landing gears. One of the common characteristics of many philosophies is that they come to no conclusions. They build roads which lead nowhere. Gossamer-thin, they evaporate, like soap bubbles, upon touching the earth. Philosophies, however, like airplanes, need landing gears. Our author brings his philosophical musings to a sharply defined and well-thought-out conclusion: "Let us hear the conclusion of the whole matter: Fear God, and keep his commandments; for this is the whole duty of man" (Eccles. 12:13).

6. We need a Savior. It is very important, as we consider a Christian philosophy of life, to understand that we need more than information or knowledge or even wisdom, no matter how wide or deep the range. We need a Savior.

7. Things eternal. Three great central doors dominate the face of a famous cathedral in Milan, Italy. Over one door are the words, "All that pleases is but for a moment." Over another are the words, "All that which troubles is but for a moment." Over the third and central door are the words, "That only is important which is eternal." The words over the central door is what the Book of Ecclesiastes is all about, and that is what any true Christian philosophy is all about.

TEACHING THE BIBLE

- *Main Idea:* Respecting and obeying God is all that keeps life from being completely futile.
- *Suggested Teaching Aim:* To lead adults to respect and obey God so they can find meaning in life

A TEACHING OUTLINE

1. *Use an illustration to introduce the Bible Study.*
2. *Use a quarter poster to overview the quarter.*
3. *Use two charts to guide the search for biblical truth.*
4. *Use discussion questions to apply the biblical truth.*
5. *Use ranking to give the truth a personal focus.*

Introduce the Bible Study

Use "The Meaning of Life" in "Applying the Bible" to introduce the Bible. Read the "Main Idea."

Search for Biblical Truth

Prepare the following quarter poster:

Wisdom for Living
Ecclesiastes, Job, Proverbs

Unit 1. When Human Wisdom Fails (Ecclesiastes, Job)

More Questions than Answers . . . . .June 7
Job's Questions. . . . . .June 14
Job's Unhelpful Friends. . . . . .June 21
God's Questions and Job's Response. . . . .June 28

Unit 2. Proverbs on Living a Disciplined Life (Proverbs)

Listen to Wisdom. . . . . July 5
Trust God . . . . July 12
Be a Good Neighbor . . . . July 19
Obey God's Law . . . . July 26

Unit 3. Two Ways—The Way of Wisdom and the Way of Foolishness (Proverbs)

Wisdom or Foolishness . . . . August 2
Hard Work and Laziness. . . . . August 9
Helpful and Harmful Speech . . . . August 16
Slow to Anger . . . . August 23
Wisdom for Family Relationships . . . . . . August 30

Display this poster all quarter. Cut an arrow from brightly colored paper; tape it beside the lesson being studied each week.

Write the following chart on a chalkboard or a large sheet of paper (members will add italicized statements):

Does Life Have Meaning?
Ecclesiastes 1:1–3

Preacher: *Son of David, King of Jerusalem [Solomon?]*

Theme: *All is vanity.*

Question: *What will you have to show for a lifetime of work?*
What is the meaning of life?

Ask members to open their Bibles to Ecclesiastes 1. (If some members do not know where to find Ecclesiastes in their Bibles, state that it is right after Psalms and Proverbs.) Ask a third of the class to discover who the *preacher* is; a third to find the *theme;* and a third to paraphrase the *question.* Explain (1) the Bible does not really mention Solomon's name, but many scholars conclude Solomon is the author; (2) the word "vanity" means empty, meaningless, absurd; and (3) the writer answered his question in verse 2 before he asked it in verse 3.

Write the following chart on a chalkboard or large sheet of paper (members will add italicized words):

Search for Meaning

Where he looked	What he found
1. *Pleasure*	*Vanity*
2. *Possessions*	*Vanity*
3. *Wisdom*	*Folly*
4. *Justice*	*Oppression*
5. *Fearing God*	*Peace*

Explain: Much of Ecclesiastes is the Preacher's description of his search for an answer to his question in 1:3. He set out to test or examine various ways in which people search for meaning for their lives.

Ask members to look at 2:1–3 and suggest the first area he examined. (Pleasure.) Write this on the chart. Ask: What did the Preacher find instead of pleasure? (Vanity.) Write that on the chart.

DISCUSS: Why do you think pleasure does not provide meaning for life?

Ask members to look at 2:10–11 and identify the second area in which the Preacher sought meaning? (Possessions.) Ask, What did he find? (Vanity.) Ask: How many times do the words "I," "my," "mine," and "myself" appear in verses 10–11? (11 times in KJV.) How would you compare this response to the story Jesus told about the rich fool in Luke 12:16–21?

DISCUSS: Why do you think possessions do not provide meaning for life?

Ask members to look at 2:12–15 and identify the third area in which the Preacher sought meaning? (Wisdom.) Ask: What did he find? (Folly.) Point out that today we would probably say he had staked his hope on education and common sense. **IN ADVANCE,** write on a large sheet of paper: "We have improved means of technology, but we have not solved any of the basic human problems that have afflicted humans since the Garden of Eden." Ask members if they agree or disagree with this statement and why.

DISCUSS: Why do you think wisdom (education) does not provide meaning for life?

Ask members to look at 4:1–3 and identify the fourth area and what he found. (Justice; oppression.)

DISCUSS: Why do you think finding meaning in justice did not work? (The world is not just.)

Ask members to look at 12:1, 13–14 and identify the fifth area and what the preacher found. (Respecting God; peace.)

DISCUSS: Why do you think he found meaning in respecting God?

Give the Truth a Personal Focus

Ask members to look at the completed chart. Read the following scale and ask members to rate themselves in each of the five areas as to how hard they are trying to find meaning in that area:

Scale

Never		Some-times		Often		Nearly Always		Always	
1	2	3	4	5	6	7	8	9	10

Ask: If Solomon, who had so much of the first four areas found they were vanity and folly, why do we still seek meaning in them? What is keeping you from seeking the meaning of life in God alone? Close in prayer that all will search for meaning in God alone and not in perishable matters.

JUNE

14

1998

Job's Questions

Basic Passages: Job 1:1–4, 8–11; 2:3–8; 3:1–4, 20–26

Focal Passages: Job 1:1–4, 8–11; 2:3–6; 3:1–3

"Why does a powerful, just, and merciful God allow good people to suffer?" Not only do theologians struggle with this question, but most people wonder about it. Many unbelievers give this as the reason for their doubt in a loving God. Most believers also ask why? when faced with this issue in a personal way. The Book of Job does not provide all the answers, but it deals more directly with the mystery of suffering than any other Bible book.

Study Aim: ***To describe Job, the dialogue between God and Satan about Job, and Job's responses to his afflictions***

STUDYING THE BIBLE

OUTLINE AND SUMMARY

I. Job's Faith and Blessings (Job 1:1–4)
- **1. Job's faith (1:1)**
- **2. Job's blessings (1:2–4)**

II. Questions by God and Satan (Job 1:8–11)
- **1. God's question to Satan (1:8)**
- **2. Satan's questions to God (1:9–11)**

III. Job's Afflictions (Job 2:3–8)
- **1. God's claim about Job (2:3)**
- **2. Satan's response to God's claim (2:4–5)**
- **3. Job's plight (2:6–8)**

IV. Job's Curses and Questions (Job 3:1–4, 20–26)
- **1. Job's curses (3:1–4)**
- **2. Job's questions (3:20–26)**

Job was a man of outstanding character and faith (1:1). He had been blessed with a close family and great wealth (1:2–4). When God asked Satan if he had considered faithful Job (1:8), Satan said that if God withdrew His blessings from Job, Job would curse God (1:9–11). When God reminded Satan that Job had maintained his faith even though he lost his blessings (2:3), Satan said that if Job's health was threatened, he would curse God (2:4–5). After God gave Satan permission to take Job's health, Job was stricken with boils and sat in ashes (2:6–8). Although at first Job responded positively, later he cursed the day of his birth (3:1–4) and expressed the desire to find rest by dying (3:20–26).

I. Job's Faith and Blessings (Job 1:1–4)

1. Job's faith (1:1)

1 There was a man in the land of Uz, whose name was Job; and that man was perfect and upright, and one that feared God, and eschewed evil.

Verse 1 emphasizes the kind of man Job was. Four characteristics of his are listed. In English, the word "perfect" carries an idea of sinless perfection that is lacking in the Hebrew word. The Hebrew word describes a person who delights in walking with God and in obeying God's law. The word "upright" describes one who faithfully adheres to God's ways and is compassionate in dealing with others. Job feared God—not in cowering terror but in his reverent and wholehearted devotion to God. He shunned evil by turning from it and refusing to participate in it (see Job 31).

2. Job's blessings (1:2–4)

2 And there were born unto him seven sons and three daughters.

3 His substance also was seven thousand sheep, and three thousand camels, and five hundred yoke of oxen, and five hundred she asses, and a very great household; so that this man was the greatest of all the men of the east.

4 And his sons went and feasted in their houses, every one his day, and sent and called for their three sisters to eat and drink with them.

Job had an ideal family. Many children were considered tokens of divine favor (Ps. 127:3–4). Sons were especially prized in that day, and Job had seven sons and three daughters. His family was close-knit and happy.

In addition, he had great wealth, which in his day was measured in livestock and servants. Job had huge numbers of sheep, camels, oxen, and donkeys. "A very great household" refers to his many servants. In fact, he was considered "the greatest of all the men of the east."

II. Questions by God and Satan (Job 1:8–11)

1. God's question to Satan (1:8)

8 And the LORD said unto Satan, Hast thou considered my servant Job, that there is none like him in the earth, a perfect and an upright man, one that feareth God, and escheweth evil?

Job 1:6–12 changes the scene from earth to the presence of God when the angels presented themselves to Him. Satan was among those who came (1:6). Satan appeared in his later biblical role as an adversary of God, accuser of human beings, and tempter of good people (Zech. 3:1–2; Rev. 12:9–10). God asked Satan if he had considered God's servant Job. "Servant" is a term of favor bestowed by God on those with whom He is pleased. God repeated to Satan the four characteristics of Job mentioned in verse 1.

2. Satan's questions to God (1:9–11)

9 Then Satan answered the LORD, and said, Doth Job fear God for nought?

10 Hast not thou made an hedge about him, and about his house, and about all that he hath on every side? thou hast

blessed the work of his hands, and his substance is increased in the land.

11 But put forth thine hand now, and touch all that he hath, and he will curse thee to thy face.

Satan's question in verse 9 is a key to the book. Satan asked if Job feared God for "nothing" ("nought") or "for no reason." Satan was convinced that neither Job nor anyone else serves God for nothing. This is spelled out in verses 10–11. In a second question, Satan asked God if He had not built a hedge of protection around Job and all that he had. He charged that Job served God because God had so richly blessed him.

Satan, therefore, proposed a test to show that he was right. He challenged God to stretch forth His hand and strike all that Job had. Satan guaranteed that Job would curse God to His face.

God did not personally strike Job's possessions, but He gave Satan permission to do so—as long as Satan did not touch Job himself (1:12). Job knew nothing of this dialogue between God and Satan; all he knew was that in one terrible day, he lost all his livestock, most of his servants, and all his beloved children (1:13–19). Although Job must have been in a state of shock, he did not curse God; to the contrary, he actually blessed God (1:20–22).

III. Job's Afflictions (Job 2:3–8)

1. God's claim about Job (2:3)

3 And the LORD said unto Satan, Hast thou considered my servant Job, that there is none like him in the earth, a perfect and an upright man, one that feareth God, and escheweth evil? and still he holdeth fast his integrity, although thou movedst me against him, to destroy him without cause.

Job 2:1–6 describes another occasion when the angels came before the Lord. Satan was there also (2:1). God asked Satan the same question He had asked in 1:8, except God added a two-pronged statement to the question. First, God said that Job had maintained his integrity in spite of the loss of his possessions. Second, God said that Satan had provoked God to ruin Job "without cause" or "for no reason" (the same word translated "for nought" in 1:9).

2. Satan's response to God's claim (2:4–5)

4 And Satan answered the LORD, and said, Skin for skin, yea, all that a man hath will he give for his life.

5 But put forth thine hand now, and touch his bone and his flesh, and he will curse thee to thy face.

What did Satan mean by "skin for skin"? The last part of verse 4 clarifies what Satan meant. Satan believed that Job would give up anything—even his faith—in order to save his life and health. Therefore, Satan proposed a second test to prove that he was right. Satan challenged God to strike Job's "bone" and "flesh." Since bones are the structure of the body and flesh the substance of the body, Satan wanted Job to be totally diseased in every way. Satan guaranteed that Job would curse God to His face.

3. Job's plight (2:6–8)

6 And the Lord said unto Satan, Behold, he is in thine hand; but save his life.

God responded by granting to Satan permission to do his worst to Job, only not to take his life. The Book of Job struggles with how God is involved in human suffering. Of course, God as Creator is ultimately responsible for everything since He made the world. In one sense, therefore, everything that happens is the will of God; however, many believers find it helpful to distinguish what God wants from what God allows. If both of these are called "the will of God," this sounds as if God wants all the evil, suffering, and injustice in the world. Therefore, some prefer to refer to the "permissive will of God." On the other hand, although God only allowed Satan to inflict Job's sufferings, God was still in control. Throughout the rest of the book, Job assumed that God stood back of what had happened. Thus Job sought to receive an answer from God; and in the end, God Himself spoke to Job.

Satan proceeded to strike Job by afflicting him with boils from head to foot (2:7). Job responded by doing what people of his day did to express deep sorrow or affliction. He went to the city ash heap and sat there. Then he scraped his sores with broken pieces of pottery (2:8). Scholars have tried unsuccessfully to narrow down Job's condition to one known disease; however, additional references to his symptoms indicate multiple problems.

Job's wife, who appears only once in the book, said: "Dost thou still retain thine integrity? curse God, and die" (2:9). However, Job responded: "Thou speakest as one of the foolish women speaketh. What? shall we receive good at the hand of God, and shall we not receive evil?" (2:10).

IV. Job's Curses and Questions (Job 3:1–4, 20–26)

1. Job's curses (3:1–4)

1 After this opened Job his mouth, and cursed his day.

2 And Job spake, and said,

3 Let the day perish wherein I was born, and the night in which it was said, There is a man child conceived.

Meanwhile three of Job's friends heard of his troubles and made plans to visit him (2:11). We don't know how much time elapsed between Job 2:7 and 2:12–13, but we do know that the three friends sat silently with Job for seven days and nights (2:12–13). Allowing time for news to reach them, for plans to be made, and for the trip itself, the total time between Job 2:7 and 3:1 may have been several months (see Job 7:3). During all that time, Job had been worn down by constant pain and inner anguish. When he finally broke his silence, he spoke very differently than he had shortly after his troubles (1:21; 2:10).

Job cursed the day of his birth and the night of his conception. The wording of verses 3–4 shows that Job wished that the day of his birth and the night of his conception could be stricken from the calendar of past events. In other words, he wished that he had never been born.

2. Job's questions (3:20–26)

Job asked why sufferers are not allowed to find rest in death (3:20–22). Applying this to himself, Job in essence asked why God, who remained hidden, had trapped Job with trouble instead of the rest he sought (3:23–26).

Readers of Job are shocked by Job's words in chapter 3. The Bible's people of faith were honest in expressing their negative feelings to God (Jer. 20:14–18; Eccles. 4:2–3). Although Job cursed the day of his birth, he stopped short of cursing God. In fact, although chapter 3 contains no direct prayers, the wording of verse 4 sounds like an indirect prayer. Job later certainly addressed his complaints to God. The Book of Job reminds us that faith is not dependent on our ability always to maintain a strong hold on God; it is trust that He always has a strong hold on us.

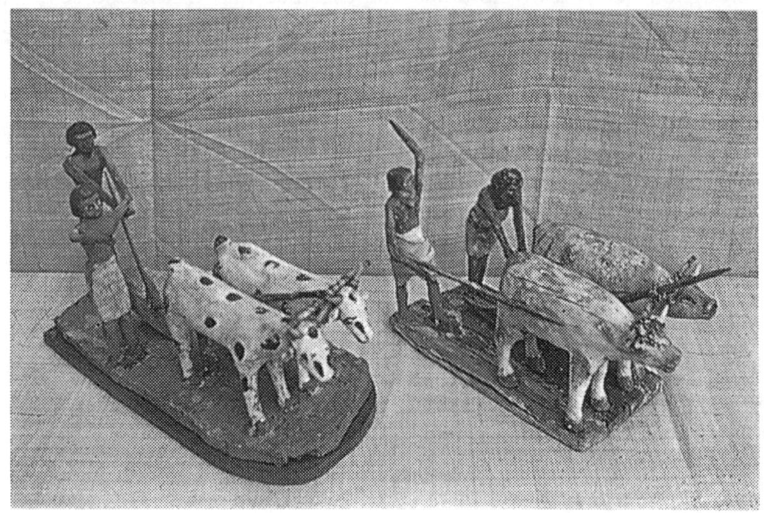

Job had five hundred oxen (Job 1:3). (Source: Holman Pictorial Collection of Biblical Antiquities, Holman Bible Publishers, Nashville, TN [Luxor, Egypt]).

APPLYING THE BIBLE

1. Why? The Book of Job is held by many to be the oldest book in the Bible, and it deals with the oldest question of humankind: "Why do the righteous suffer?" Jesus once told us that the day would come when we would ask Him nothing (John 16:23). But until then we ask, "Why?" In fact, this may be the most human question of all. On a tombstone in a German cemetery is one word, "Varum," which means "Why?" There must be an interesting story behind that tombstone. My guess is that Job would have understood. In any case, Job raises that same one-word question poignantly in his book.

2. From God's perspective. Before anyone criticizes God for His dealings with us, we should remember that we cannot judge, rightly, about all of God's actions unless we are thoroughly acquainted with all of God's problems. As we talked about these things one day, a young friend of mine quietly said, without any dishonor to God, "Maybe it ain't no picnic being God."

3. Incorruptible. The key element in Job's character, made manifest in his response to his trials, was his total incorruptibility. He did not let the pressures on his flesh cause him to disown or deny God. Sadly, Satan's observation would have been enough to cause most of us to crumble: "Put forth thine hand now, and touch his bone and his flesh, and he will curse thee to thy face" (Job 2:5).

4. Bargaining with God. A modern American media mogul turned from his childhood faith in God because, he said, he prayed often for God to spare the life of his cancer-ridden sister, and God did not. Have you ever tried to make an if-You-do-this-I'll-serve-You-and-if-not-I-won't deal with God?

5. Is God in control? Rabbi Harold Kushner wrote a book about Job called *When Bad Things Happen to Good People.* Kushner takes the position that God wants to help us in tragic situations, but He simply can't at times for many reasons. In fact, Kushner doesn't believe much of the Book of Job because he doesn't think God would have allowed such a good man to suffer as Job did. (But remember Jesus!) His counsel? "There are some things God does not control."[1] Notice that Kushner does not say God *can't* control but *won't;* elsewhere he says He is simply unable to control. Kushner continues, "Are you capable of forgiving and loving God even when you have found out that He is not perfect? . . . Can you learn to love and forgive Him despite His limitations?"[2] How would you counter Kushner's view of God? Is it possible that God can use suffering? Can He ever redeem it? Even if it doesn't have meaning to us, could it have meaning to Him? Or to others? And even if we don't understand what it means now, might it make sense to us when we view it from heaven's perspective? How does Romans 8:28 come into the picture? How did Paul's suffering experience, recorded in 2 Corinthians 12, cause him to grow? (By the way, the professed Christian theologian Edgar Sheffield Brightman, like Rabbi Kushner, argued that God is finite and, therefore, cannot control certain situations and circumstances.)

6. The uses of adversity. People once believed that certain frogs had jewels imbedded in their heads and that the frogs protected the jewels by their ability to emit poison to any who would take the stones. This explains Shakespeare's lines in *As You Like It:*

> Sweet are the uses of adversity;
> Which like the toad, ugly and venomous,
> Wears yet a precious jewel in his head. (2.1.12–14)

Has God used adversities to conform your life more to His plan?

TEACHING THE BIBLE

- *Main Idea:* God often allows circumstances to happen that are not His will for us.
- *Suggested Teaching Aim:* To lead adults to state how they will trust in God even in the midst of conflict

A TEACHING OUTLINE

1. Use a quotation to introduce and conclude the Bible study.
2. Enlist two members to summarize the background material.
3. Use the chalkboard and listing to help members search for biblical truth.
4. Use discussion questions to relate the biblical material to members' lives.
5. Use a quotation to give the truth a personal focus.

Introduce the Bible Study

IN ADVANCE, write on a large sheet of paper: "Why does a powerful, just, and merciful God allow good people to suffer?" Ask members to respond. Suggest that this was really Job's question, too, and that the lesson will help to provide an answer.

Search for Biblical Truth

Enlist two readers to read the summary statements in "Outline and Summary" alternately to summarize this long background passage.

On a chalkboard or a large sheet of paper write: *Job's Attributes.* Ask members to turn to Job 1:2–4 and to list the four ways Job is described. List these on the chalkboard. Use "Studying the Bible" to explain the terms. Then write: *Job's Blessings* and ask members to list all of Job's blessings found in these verses. Write these on the chalkboard.

Ask half the class to find and paraphrase God's questions and half to find and paraphrase Satan's questions in 1:8–11.

DISCUSS: Why do you serve God?

Ask: What was God's affirmation about Job in 2:3? How does it differ from the affirmation in 1:8? Write on a chalkboard the following bold statements (members will add italicized information):

Satan's first challenge:	*Does Job fear God for nought?*
God's first response:	*Take all but Job's body.*
Satan's second challenge:	*People will give all they have to save their lives.*
God's second response:	*Take all but Job's life.*

Ask members to contrast Satan's first and second challenges and God's first and second responses. Use "Studying the Bible" to explain difficult terms.

DISCUSS: How do you distinguish between what God permits and what He wants?

On a chalkboard write: *Job's Response.* Ask members to read 3:1–4 and to identify how Job responded to his afflictions. (With curses and questions.) Ask: How did this differ from the way he responded to the loss of his property and possessions? Why do you think Job stopped short of cursing God?

DISCUSS: How do you respond to situations you cannot control?

Give the Truth a Personal Focus

Call attention to the question you asked at the beginning. (Why does a powerful, just, and merciful God allow good people to suffer?) Ask members to turn to persons near them and discuss this and then share responses with the whole class. (Or you can do this as a whole class.)

Ask members to share how they will trust in God even in the midst of conflict when they see no sense in what is happening.

---

1. Harold Kushner, *When Bad Things Happen to Good People*, 45.
2. Ibid., 148.

JUNE

21

1998

Job's Unhelpful Friends

Basic Passages: Job 2:11; 4:1–7; 8:1–7; 11:1–6; 13:1–4; 23:1–7

Focal Passages: Job 2:11; 4:1, 6–7; 8:1–6; 13:1–4

Sometimes well-meaning friends do more harm than good when trying to comfort the suffering. Job's friends went to comfort him, and ended up accusing him of sins he had not committed. Their belief in earthly retribution and rewards led them to assume that Job's sufferings meant that he had sinned. Their accusations led Job to lash back at them and to yearn for vindication by God.

➧ **Study Aim:** ***To summarize the main points made by Job's friends and how Job responded***

STUDYING THE BIBLE

OUTLINE AND SUMMARY

I. Well-Meaning Friends (Job 2:11)

II. Hurting Rather than Helping (Job 4:1–7; 8:1–7; 11:1–6)

1. Feeble comfort (4:1–6)

2. Crux of the issue (4:7)

3. Insensitive rebukes (8:1–4; 11:1–6)

4. Call to repent (8:5–7)

III. Job's Responses (Job 13:1–4; 23:1–7)

1. Rebuke of the friends (13:1–2, 4)

2. Desire to speak to God (13:3; 23:1–7)

Job's three friends came to comfort him (2:11). Following Job's words in chapter 3, one of the friends made a feeble attempt to combine comfort with mild rebuke (4:1–6). He also stated the crux of the disagreement with Job: that the righteous are always blessed in this life (4:7). Two later speakers delivered insensitive rebukes to Job (8:1–4; 11:1–6). One of these also called Job to seek God and become upright (8:5–7). Job accused them of lying and being worthless physicians (13:1–2, 4). Job concentrated on his yearning to be able to present his case to God (13:3; 23:1–7).

I. Well-Meaning Friends (Job 2:11)

11 Now when Job's three friends heard of all this evil that was come upon him, they came every one from his own place; Eliphaz the Temanite, and Bildad the Shuhite, and Zophar the Naamathite: for they had made an appointment together to come to mourn with him and to comfort him.

These three were real friends of Job. Their actions in verse 11 testify to their concern about him. The fact that they later hurt rather than helped him does not change the fact that in the beginning they were well-meaning friends who cared about Job. They came to sympathize with him and to try to comfort him. The three friends were Eliphaz (el ih FAZ) the Temanite (TEE muhn ight), Bildad (BIL dad) the Shuhite (SHOO ight), and Zophar (ZOH fur) the Naamathite (NAY uh muh thight).

When the friends first caught sight of Job, they did not recognize him. They wept, tore their clothes, put dust on their heads, and sat silently with Job for seven days and seven nights (2:12–13).

II. Hurting Rather than Helping (Job 4:1–7; 8:1–7; 11:1–6)

1. Feeble comfort (4:1–6)

1 Then Eliphaz the Temanite answered and said.

The friends were still sitting with Job when Job spoke the bitter words of chapter 3. This caused them to break their silence. Job 4–27, the bulk of the Book of Job, records three cycles of speeches. In the first two cycles, Eliphaz, Bildad, and Zophar spoke with responses from Job after each one spoke. In the third cycle, Eliphaz and Bildad spoke; but Zophar did not. Job 4:1–7; 8:1–7; and 11:1–6 constitute the opening of the speech of each friend during the first cycle.

6 Is not this thy fear, thy confidence, thy hope, and the uprightness of thy ways?

Eliphaz began as gently as he could by asking Job if he would be grieved if they spoke with him. He indicated that he could not remain silent any longer (4:2). Eliphaz affirmed Job as one who in the past had instructed others and strengthened the weak. Eliphaz was implying that he had done what they were trying to do for him (4:3–4). Verse 5 is a gentle rebuke. Job had helped others; but when trouble came to him, Job became impatient and troubled.

Job had been renowned for his fear of God and upright character (1:1, 8; 2:3). Eliphaz asked Job if these qualities should not provide him confidence and hope in his troubles. Job's curses and questions did not seem to Eliphaz to be appropriate for a person known for fear of God and upright character.

2. Crux of the issue (4:7)

7 Remember, I pray thee, who ever perished, being innocent? or where were the righteous cut off?

Eliphaz's two questions got to the heart of the issue that divided the friends from Job. He asked whether an innocent person had perished or a righteous person had ever been cut off or destroyed? Eliphaz expected an innocent or righteous person to live a long life.

The three friends believed in the orthodox position of the day—earthly rewards for the righteous, and suffering and death for sinners. Eliphaz later admitted that trouble sometimes comes to good people, but it passes and does not destroy the person (5:17–27). However, continued suffering and words such as Job spoke in chapter 3 were not good signs. Although Eliphaz in his first speech did not accuse Job of sin, he laid the groundwork for it.

Job no doubt had agreed with this theology until his experience with terrible, continuous suffering. Job never claimed absolute sinlessness, but he knew that he had not done anything to deserve that depth of suffering. Thus, his experience led him to question the view so smugly set forth by the three would-be comforters.

A basic premise of their theology was that this life is the arena in which rewards or punishments are experienced. The people of that day had not received the revelation of eternal life that Christians have. Death to them was at best a shadowy existence (see Job 10:20–22; 14:7–12; 17:13–16). Later Job's experience led him to express a wistful hope that God would vindicate him in an afterlife (14:13–14; 19:23–27). This wistful hope became a foreshadowing of the confident hope we have through the resurrection of Jesus Christ from the dead (1 Pet. 1:3–5).

3. Insensitive rebukes (8:1–4; 11:1–6)

1 Then answered Bildad the Shuhite, and said,

2 How long wilt thou speak these things? and how long shall the words of thy mouth be like a strong wind?

3 Doth God pervert judgment? or doth the Almighty pervert justice?

4 If thy children have sinned against him, and he have cast them away for their transgressions.

Bildad had listened to Job's response to Eliphaz (Job 6–7). Although Job had requested pity from his friends (6:14) and expressed a willingness to listen to them (6:24), he continued to complain about his undeserved sufferings. Bildad expressed frustration with having to endure Job's long, windy speech.

Verse 3 reinforced the view of earthly justice already mentioned by Eliphaz in 4:7. Like Eliphaz, Bildad used two questions to make the same basic point. Eliphaz had stressed that the righteous never perish; Bildad emphasized that God never perverts justice. Job also believed in the justice of God; however, his experience was forcing him to reexamine how and when God's justice is expressed.

Verse 4 shows how insensitive the would-be comforters could be. Imagine saying this to a father grieving over the death of all his children. The circumstances of their deaths led Bildad to assume that they were being punished for their sins. Job himself had done all he could to ensure that his sons had not sinned; and to be sure they were right with God, Job offered sacrifices for them (1:5).

Later when Zophar spoke for the first time, he also delivered a harsh, insensitive rebuke to Job. He accused Job not only of too much talk but also of lying and mockery (11:1–3). He paraphrased Job's position as a claim to be pure and clean in God's eyes (11:4). Zophar yearned for God to reply to such lies by telling Job that he was not suffering more than he deserved, but less (11:5–6).

4. Call to repent (8:5–7)

5 If thou wouldest seek unto God betimes, and make thy supplication to the Almighty;

6 If thou wert pure and upright; surely now he would awake for thee, and make the habitation of thy righteousness prosperous.

Returning to Bildad's first speech, he moved from a condemnation of Job's children to a call for Job to seek the Lord. As far as Bildad was concerned, the sinful children were beyond hope because their deaths sealed their punishment. Job, however, was still living. This meant to Bildad that there was still hope that he had not gone as far in sin as those who had paid the ultimate price of death. Like Eliphaz (5:8), Bildad still held out hope for Job.

Bildad urged Job to seek the Lord with soft words of conciliation rather than the strong words of complaint he had been using. If Job was as pure and upright as he claimed, God would surely restore him to health and prosperity. In fact, verse 7 says that Job would be even more blessed than before. The wording of verse 6 probably means that although Bildad did not think Job was pure and upright, he held out hope that he might again become so.

III. Job's Responses (Job 13:1–4; 23:1–7)

1. Rebuke of the friends (13:1–2, 4)

1 Lo, mine eye hath seen all this, mine ear hath heard and understood it.

2 What ye know, the same do I know also: I am not inferior unto you.

4 But ye are forgers of lies, ye are all physicians of no value.

This is part of Job's response to Zophar in the first cycle of speeches. Verses 1–2, 4 express one of two themes that run throughout Job's speeches: (1) he rebuked his friends, and (2) he yearned for an opportunity to receive vindication from God. As the cycles of speeches continued, Job became more and more impatient with his friends. He had hoped they would listen to him, sympathize with him, and help him. Instead, they repeated ideas he already knew but was being forced to question by his experience. Thus, Job claimed that they had said nothing that he didn't already know. His theology and wisdom was in no way inferior to theirs.

Verse 4 is a strong rebuke of the would-be comforters. Zophar had accused Job of lying (11:3). Job now accused them of lying. He used a word meaning "smear" to describe their lies. They had smeared or whitewashed the difficulties of explaining his plight with lies. They did this to maintain their own positions as flawless. Job also accused them of being worthless physicians or quacks. They offered remedies that did not help or heal.

2. Desire to speak to God (13:3; 23:1–7)

3 Surely I would speak to the Almighty, and I desire to reason with God.

As the dialogue progressed, Job expressed strongly and repeatedly his desire to be able to present his case before God. He felt sure that God would vindicate him as a righteous man, not as the sinner his friends accused him of being.

Job 23:1–7 is Job's speech to Eliphaz in the final cycle. His bitter complaint caused him to want to find God and present his case to

God (23:1–5). Job briefly considered the possibility that God might not take his side, but he rejected that in favor of the assumption that God would vindicate him (23:6–7). Job's problem, however, was that God remained silent and hidden; so Job could not find Him (23:8–9). Then in Job 23:10, Job rose to one of the highest peaks of faith in the book. Although he couldn't find God, Job believed God knew all about him and that God was refining him so that he would become like gold purified in the fire.

Outline of Job

I. Prologue: Dialogue between God and Satan. Job's troubles and his initial responses (Job 1–2)
II. Job curses the day of his birth (Job 3)
III. First Cycle of Speeches: Eliphaz, Job, Bildad, Job, Zophar, Job (Job 4–14)
IV. Second Cycle of Speeches: Same order as first (Job 15–21)
V. Third Cycle of Speeches: Eliphaz, Job, Bildad, Job (Job 22–28)
VI. Job sums up his case (Job 29–31)
VII. Elihu speaks (Job 32–37)
VIII. God answers Job. Job's first response. God continues His answer: God continues His answer. Job's second response (Job 38:1–42:6).
IX. Epilogue: God commends Job and condemns his friends. Job prays for his friends, and God restores Job (Job 42:7–21).

APPLYING THE BIBLE

1. Better or worse? Job's friends meant well, no doubt, but they brought great pain in his life. I once asked a hospital administrator if he liked seeing pastors entering the hospital to visit patients. His answer was, "Well, it depends!" Then he explained. When some pastors left, he said, the patients had better attitudes and a more positive outlook on life. But when others left, it was the reverse.

2. Angelic visitors. I once heard an older pastor say about visiting hurting people: "Make your visits like those of the angels: brief, bright, and bearing good news!" Job's friends failed that threefold test—miserably. Their visits were neither brief nor bright, and they bore little truly good news.

3. Last request. According to one story, a pastor was visiting a hospital patient and, during the visit, the patient feebly called for a piece of paper on which to write a note. The pastor, supposing he was putting down his dying words, was moved by the seriousness of the moment. The patient, gasping his last breath, handed the note to the pastor, then expired. The note read, "Would you please not stand on my oxygen hose?" Job's well-meaning friends were ancient practitioners of the no-oxygen approach to medicine!

4. Comforting the afflicted. The Bible says that "a brother is born for adversity" (Prov. 17:17). Here are three rules for encouraging sufferers:

- Be there for them;
- Don't give glib "canned" answers; and
- Do assure them of your love and commitment to them.

Of course, they need answers, but answers are much easier to assimilate after the throes of the traumatic experience have been allowed to pass.

5. Vertical and horizontal. The French sociologist Emile Durkheim (1858–1917) saw the essential role of religion as horizontal. Rather than focusing on our vertical relationship with God, he focused on our horizontal relationship with other people. Durkheim said religion's essential role is to produce "social cohesiveness"; it is a social force that enables fellow sufferers to go through life's difficult passages, such as the passages from youth into adulthood, marriage, parenting, aging, and death. Biblical faith includes both the vertical (our relationship to God) and the horizontal (our relationship to other people). The Ten Commandments begin with the vertical and move on to the horizontal.

6. Thoughts on advice.

- "The worst men often give the best advice" (P. J. Bailey).
- "When Thales [an early Greek philosopher] was asked what was difficult, he said, 'To know one's self.' And what was easy, 'To advise another'" (Diogenes Laertius).
- "Advice is cheap."
- "It is easy when we are in prosperity to give advice to the afflicted" (Aeschylus).
- "Advice is like snow; the softer it falls the longer it dwells upon, and the deeper it sinks into the mind" (Samuel Taylor Coleridge).

TEACHING THE BIBLE

- *Main Idea:* Job's experience with his unhelpful friends can help us avoid hurting people by our actions.
- *Suggested Teaching Aim:* To lead adults to identify ways they can help those who are hurting

A TEACHING OUTLINE

1. Use an illustration to introduce the Bible study.

2. Use a listening assignment for the class.

3. Use a true-false test to help members search for biblical truth.

4. Use a group activity to give the truth a personal focus.

JUNE

21

1998

Introduce the Bible Study

Use "Last request" in "Applying the Bible" to introduce the Bible study. Suggest that today's lesson will help members identify ways they can help those who are hurting.

Search for Biblical Truth

Distribute paper and pencils to members. Ask half the class to listen for what Job's three friends did that was right; ask the other half of the class to listen for what Job's friends did that was wrong.

Read or briefly summarize the seven summary statements in "Outline and Summary" since the Scripture passages cover a great deal of material.

Read the following True-False statements or photocopy this pretest-posttest and give a copy to each person:

		Pretest Posttest		
T	F	1. Eliphaz, Bildad, and Zophar came to see Job.	T	F
T	F	2. Job helped others; when trouble came to him Job became impatient and troubled.	T	F
T	F	3. The three friends believed in the generally accepted belief of their day: earthly rewards for the righteous, and suffering and death for sinners.	T	F
T	F	4. Job claimed he was absolutely sinless.	T	F
T	F	5. Job's experience led him to question the view his would-be comforters set forth.	T	F
T	F	6. Bildad said Job's children had died unjustly.	T	F
T	F	7. Bildad said if Job was as pure and upright as he claimed, God would surely restore his health and prosperity.	T	F
T	F	8. Job's friends accused him of being a worthless physician or quack.	T	F
T	F	9. Job pleaded for a chance to present his case before God.	T	F
T	F	10. Job was angry because God remained silent.	T	F
(Answers: **1.** T; **2.** T; **3.** T; **4.** F; **5.** T; **6.** F; **7.** T; **8.** F; **9.** T; **10.** T.)				

Use the above ten statements as an outline for a lecture. Ask the question, and call for the correct response. Use "Studying the Bible" to explain the setting of each statement. After you have done this, ask members to take the posttest to see if they can answer them correctly.

Give the Truth a Personal Focus

On a chalkboard or a large sheet of paper, write *Right* and *Wrong*. Ask members to share what they found Job's friends did that was right and wrong. The following are suggested responses only:

Right

They came.
They listened (at least at first).
They believed God could help.
They were hurt when they saw Job's pain.

Wrong

They assumed they knew God's mind.
They assumed that their position was right.
They claimed a special revelation from God.
The orthodox position was wrong.
They were absolutely convinced that there was a direct relationshipbetween sin and suffering.

They didn't tell Job anything he didn't already know.

Ask members to take the wrong actions and make them positive statements. (God's actions are sometimes beyond our understanding.) Ask members to look at the list and develop a checklist of steps they can take to help those who are hurting. Use "Comforting the afflicted" in "Applying the Bible." Close in prayer that members will be especially sensitive this week to helping those who feel alienated from God.

JUNE

28

1998

God's Questions and Job's Response

Basic Passages: Job 38:1–7; 42:1–6, 10

Focal Passages: Job 38:1–7; 42:1–6, 10

Zophar asked God to speak in order to tell Job that his sins were greater than his punishment (11:5–6). Job called on God to reveal Himself so that Job could present his case before God. Job fully expected that this would result in God vindicating him as innocent (23:1–7). When God finally spoke to Job, what He said and how He said it surprised both Job and his friends.

➧ **Study Aim:** *To explain Job's responses to God's questions*

STUDYING THE BIBLE

OUTLINE AND SUMMARY

I. **God's Questions to Job (Job 38:1–7)**
   1. **The Lord answered Job (38:1)**
   2. **Words without knowledge (38:2)**
   3. **Unanswerable questions (38:3–7)**

II. **Job's Responses to God (Job 42:1–6, 10)**
   1. **Let God be God (42:1–4)**
   2. **Testified to his personal experience (42:5)**
   3. **Repented (42:6)**
   4. **Prayed for his friends (42:10)**

The Lord answered Job out of a whirlwind (38:1). God accused Job of distorting His purpose by speaking out of ignorance (38:2). God then asked Job to answer a series of unanswerable questions (38:3–7). Job responded by affirming God's power and purpose as he confessed his own ignorance (42:1–4). Job testified that he had formerly known only what he had heard about God, but now he had seen God (42:5). Job repented (42:6). After Job prayed for his friends, God restored his prosperity (42:10).

I. God's Questions to Job (Job 38:1–7)

1. The Lord answered Job (38:1)

1 Then the LORD answered Job out of the whirlwind, and said,

Job's final speech was an eloquent defense of his innocence and a plea for a hearing before God. Job was so confident of his innocence that he would approach God as if Job were a prince (Job 26–31; see 31:37).

God answered Job out of a whirlwind. The Old Testament often describes God revealing Himself in a storm (Exod. 19:16–19; Ps. 18:7–13; Nah. 2:3–5). Such revelations created a sense of awe among those who witnessed them. Job had asked for an orderly hearing before God in a courtroom setting; instead, God answered Job out of a whirlwind. On the other hand, the very fact that God answered the suffering Job was a sign of divine grace. God did not come to Job to declare him righteous as Job had requested; however, God's coming to Job showed His concern for Job.

2. Words without knowledge (38:2)

2 Who is this that darkeneth counsel by words without knowledge?

The word "counsel" referred to the wisdom that permeated God's creation and government of the universe. God's "counsel" is His providence—His wise, just, and gracious purpose. God accused Job of distorting His purpose by speaking many words out of ignorance.

In looking at this verse and later verses in which Job repented, we need to keep in mind what God said in 42:7: God accused the three friends of not speaking right about God as Job had done. In what sense was Job right, and in what sense was he wrong? He was right to defend his innocence against the wild accusations of his friends. He was right to take his case to God. He was wrong to question how God ran His universe.

3. Unanswerable questions (38:3–7)

3 Gird up now thy loins like a man; for I will demand of thee, and answer thou me.

4 Where wast thou when I laid the foundations of the earth? declare, if thou hast understanding.

5 Who hath laid the measures thereof, if thou knowest? or who hath stretched the line upon it?

6 Whereupon are the foundations thereof fastened? or who laid the corner stone thereof;

7 When the morning stars sang together, and all the sons of God shouted for joy?

Job had been demanding that God answer his questions. In verse 3, God demanded that Job answer God's questions. Throughout verses 4–6, God used the figure of erecting a building to picture His creative work. God asked Job where he was when God created the earth. Of course, no human being was there when God began His creative work. God asked Job to tell who laid the foundations for the creation of the universe and performed the other steps in building. God asked Job if he knew how the universe was created. God described the rejoicing when the creation was completed as comparable to laying the cornerstone of a building. When that happened, the stars sang together, and the angels shouted for joy.

II. Job's Responses to God (Job 42:1–6, 10)

1. Let God be God (42:1–4)

1 Then Job answered the LORD, and said,

2 I know that thou canst do every thing, and that no thought can be withholden from thee.

3 Who is he that hideth counsel without knowledge? therefore have I uttered that I understood not; things too wonderful for me, which I knew not.

4 Hear, I beseech thee, and I will speak: I will demand of thee, and declare thou unto me.

God continued to ask Job questions about the wisdom of God in creation (Job 38–39). Then God asked Job to answer if he could (40:1–2). Job confessed that he had already said too much; he was humbled into silence (40:3–5). Then God continued with a barrage of questions about God's governing of the universe (Job 40:6–41:34). Job's first response (other than 40:3–5) is in 42:1–4.

Verse 2 begins with an affirmation of the power of God to do anything. The last part of verse 2 reads as if Job was saying that no human thought can be hid from God. That is surely true, but it was probably not what Job meant here. The word translated "thought" means "purpose." The word translated "withholden" means "thwarted." Thus Job was probably saying that humans cannot thwart the powerful purpose of God. Job never doubted God's power, but he had wondered about His purpose. Now he affirmed both His power and His purpose.

Verse 3 begins by quoting God's question about Job in 38:2. The last part of verse 3 is Job's confession that God was right in accusing him of talking about things he didn't understand. Verse 4 is a quotation of God's earlier challenge to Job in 40:7. Perhaps by quoting God's challenge, Job was saying to God that he had gotten the message God was trying to communicate to him.

2. Testified of his personal experience (42:5)

5 I have heard of thee by the hearing of the ear: but now mine eye seeth thee.

This may be the key verse in Job. "Hearing" refers to "hearsay." Job was referring to the teachings and traditions he had heard about God. The three friends repeated what Job had always heard about God—a mixture of truth and distortion. Now, however, Job was not dependent on what he had only heard about God, because Job had experienced a personal encounter with God. He spoke of this as seeing God in contrast to merely hearing about God.

God had revealed Himself to Job, but much mystery about God always remains even when God reveals Himself. Job's inability to answer God's questions reminds us that humans can never fully fathom the ways of Almighty God (Isa. 55:8–9). We cannot know everything about God, but we can know God. Job still had unanswered questions. He was still sitting on that ash heap with no explanation from God about why he was suffering. Yet the sufferer seemed satisfied because now he had seen God.

Job's response in verse 5 proves that Satan was wrong when he insisted that Job served God only because God had blessed him. Job was still on the ash heap, but he was affirming his trust in God. Job did not worship God only because of the material gifts God had given him; instead, Job worshiped God for God's own sake.

3. Repented (42:6)

6 Wherefore I abhor myself, and repent in dust and ashes.

Because God later condemned the three friends and commended Job for speaking the truth, we must be careful as we seek to explain why Job repented. Job 42:7 shows that Job had spoken the truth about God while his friends had not. Of course, not everything they said was wrong, and not everything Job said was right; however, Job was right to maintain his innocence of doing anything that caused God to punish him with his afflictions. The friends were wrong to insist that Job must have sinned grievously to receive such sufferings.

But of what then did Job repent? Job had already confessed his ignorance of God's ways about which he had too much to say. Out of ignorance, he had at times questioned the justice and love of God. In a sense, his chief sin was that he still basically agreed with his friends', assumptions: a just God must reward a person's good life with material blessings and shield him from the kind of sufferings Job was enduring. Job's plea was that God grant him a fair hearing. Job assumed there had been some kind of mix-up for such a man as he to be suffering. Therefore, if he could get God's attention and present the facts of his righteous life, God would vindicate him and restore his blessings. His sin, therefore, was in claiming divine blessings based on his own goodness.

4. Prayed for his friends (42:10)

10 And the LORD turned the captivity of Job, when he prayed for his friends: also the LORD gave Job twice as much as he had before.

God told Eliphaz that His wrath was directed against the three friends of Job because they did not speak what was right about God, as Job had done (42:7). God instructed Eliphaz to get Job to go with them as they offered burnt offerings for their sins, and God promised that His servant Job would pray for them (42:8). They did as God commanded (42:9), and Job prayed for them (42:10).

Verse 10 connects Job's prayer for his friends with the end of his sufferings and a restoration of material blessings. The strong implication is that Job's willingness to pray for these men marked the beginning of new life for him. Praying for these three tormentors would not have been an easy thing for Job to do; however, after Job had a personal experience with God, he was able to fulfill this difficult task.

Some Bible students have problems with Job receiving back his material blessings, in fact, being even more blessed. These students feel that such an ending undercuts the book's message of trust in God by righteous sufferers. However, keep these three things in mind:

1. Job's restoration was not a reward for his good life. The restoration, like the original blessings themselves, were gifts of divine grace.

2. The opening dialogues between God and Satan made clear that Job's sufferings were a test, therefore likely to be temporary. Job himself had glimpsed this possibility in 23:10. The Book of Job does not deny the doctrine of retribution, but it does clearly show that not all sufferers are being punished for sins. Jesus denied that suffering is always punish-

ment for sin (John 9:1–3). The Book of Job was a step in divine revelation about ultimate rewards and punishments after death, not in this life.

3. The Book of Job does not remove but intensifies the mystery of human suffering. When suffering comes, people continue to ask, "Why?" and "Why me?" We remain ignorant of the mystery of divine providence and human suffering; however, Job shows us that faith is not based on finding answers to all our questions; it is based on trusting the justice and goodness of God in spite of circumstances that seem to deny these realities. The cross and resurrection provide help for us that Job did not have. The cross reveals that God suffers with us and for us; and the resurrection reveals that God has the final word over suffering, sin, and death. Job thus sets the background for Paul's affirmation in Romans 8:28. Even though we can't explain why trouble comes, we know that God is at work and will bring good out of evil situations.

APPLYING THE BIBLE

1. God's questions. Job asked God many questions in the book that bears his name, but the tables turned when God began to ask Job questions. We like to ask God questions, but God has a right to ask us questions too! Too many people assume the questioning is always a one-way deal, but—from one cover of the Bible to the other—we are told that judgment is coming, judgment in which God will ask the questions.

2. No contest. God asked Job ten questions about the natural order (38:4–38) and nine questions about animals (38:39–39:30). Every question produced a profound sense of awe—and ignorance—in Job. It is always proper, in regard to life's mysteries, to declare bankruptcy on ourselves and solvency on God because that is precisely the situation! And we need to try to do so early in the relationship!

3. Blasphemy. Eumonius, an early bishop, once said that he knew more about God than God knew about Himself! If that sentence was said in jest, it was blasphemy; but, apparently, the bishop was serious, so it was blasphemy raised to the tenth power!

4. Hand-to-hand combat. God told Job, "Gird up thy loins now like a man." That was God's invitation to the ancient sport of belt-wrestling. God was saying to him, "You wish to wrestle; let's have at it!" The Hebrew word for "man" here is the unusual "geber," which refers to man in his strength, man as warrior, and man as combatant. Again, that evidences the fact that God accepted Job's persistent challenge for hand-to-hand combat!

5. Human pride. Shakespeare, in the play *Measure for Measure,* wrote these memorable lines about human pride:

> But man, proud man,
> Dress'd in a little brief authority,
> Most ignorant of what he's most assur'd
> (His glassy essence), like an angry ape
> Plays such fantastic tricks before high heaven
> As makes the angels weep. (2.2.117)

6. Repentance and relationship. The good news is that Job repented of his arrogance ("Wherefore I abhor myself, and repent in dust and ashes" [42:6]), and, as a result, God said He would accept "My servant Job" (42:8). Repentance is always indispensable to any meaningful relationship to God.

7. Dangerous questions. Are there persistent questions you are asking God—in an angry and cynical attitude? Do these questions have to do with the way you think God has mistreated you? What are the dangers of harboring such questions in your spirit?

8. Solid rock. At the end of his experience with God, Job would have thoroughly understood the great line in the hymn "The Solid Rock":

When darkness seems to hide His face,
I rest on His unchanging grace.[1]

TEACHING THE BIBLE

- *Main Idea:* Job's questions and God's answers show God's concern for us in the midst of conflict.
- *Suggested Teaching Aim:* To lead adults to identify ways God has cared for them in the midst of crises

A TEACHING OUTLINE

1. Use a hymn to introduce the Bible study.
2. Use charts, lecture, and Bible searching to guide the search for biblical truth.
3. Use testimony to give the truth a personal focus.

Introduce the Bible Study

Sing or read the words to the first and second stanzas of the hymn "The Solid Rock." Suggest that the words "When darkness seems to hide His face, I rest on His unchanging grace" would summarize Job's feelings at the end of His experience with God, but certainly not at the beginning. Today's lesson will help us see how Job came from accusing God to resting in His grace.

Search for Biblical Truth

IN ADVANCE, on a chalkboard or a large sheet of paper, write (omit italicized phrases):

What Job Wanted	What Job Got
1. Orderly court hearing	*God in a tornado*
2. Vindication of his innocence	*Confounded by God*
3. Answers to his questions	*Meeting with God*

To set the scene for this lesson, point out the three things Job wanted; then, let members suggest what he got.

JUNE
28
1998

Ask a member to read Job 38:1. Ask: How many times in the Bible can you recall that God appeared in a storm? (Exod. 19:16–19; Ps. 18:7–13; Nah. 2:3–5; 1 Kings 19:1–18 are examples.)

Read Job 38:2 and 42:7. Say: In 38:2, God criticized Job for talking when he didn't know what he was talking about. Yet, in 42:7 God said Job had spoken the truth. Ask: What did Job do and say that was right? (To defend his innocence and to take his case to God.) What did he do wrong? (Questioned how God ran His universe.)

Read 38:3–7. Say: These are just examples of some of the questions God asked Job in 38:3–39:30. All the questions have to do with how God created the world and cares for it; all were questions Job could not answer.

Read 42:1–6, 10. Ask members to paraphrase these verses and/or summarize them in one sentence. (Something like: Job said he was foolish for presuming to question God.) **IN ADVANCE,** make a poster of 42:5. Suggest to members that this verse may be the key verse in Job. Read the following statement and ask members why they agree or disagree: "In a sense, his chief sin was that he still basically agreed with his friends', assumptions: a just God must reward a person's good life with material blessings and shield him from the kind of sufferings Job was enduring."

Write the following on a chalkboard. Members may add other lessons Job learned:

What Job Learned about God from This Encounter

- God cares.
- God is more powerful than we are.
- God does reveal Himself to us.
- God does not reveal all His mystery to us.
- God was worthy of worship for His own sake, not for what He gave in material goods.
- God is gracious.
- God asks us to forgive those who have wronged us.

Use the three statements in "Studying the Bible" to explain why God restored Job's material blessings.

Give the Truth a Personal Focus

Ask: What lessons can we learn from Job? (Many, but primarily that God does care for us in our conflicts.) Ask members to suggest ways God has cared for them in their conflicts in the past. Ask: If God has done this in the past, what are the possibilities of His doing this in the future? Read the words of 42:5 from the poster. Remind members that they have seen God in the face of Jesus.

---

1. Edward Mote, "The Solid Rock," *Baptist Hymnal* (Nashville: Convention Press, 1956), 283.

Listen to Wisdom

Basic Passage: Proverbs 2:1–15
Focal Passage: Proverbs 2:1–15

When we think of a proverb, we usually think of a short, folksy saying that states some sage advice or commonplace truth in a pithy, memorable way. We have lots of proverbs in our own language: "Don't count your chickens before they hatch." "The early bird gets the worm." "A rolling stone gathers no moss." The Book of Proverbs contains many comparable sayings, but it also contains some words of wisdom in discourse form. These wisdom discourses are found primarily in Proverbs 1–9. Proverbs 2:1–15 is a discourse on the blessings of listening to wisdom.

➧ **Study Aim:** *To define wisdom and to name three blessings of listening to wisdom*

STUDYING THE BIBLE

OUTLINE AND SUMMARY

I. Call to Listen to Wisdom (Prov. 2:1–4)
II. Blessings of Listening to Wisdom (Prov. 2:5–15)
  1. Fear and knowledge of God (vv. 5–8)
  2. Moral discernment (vv. 9–11)
  3. Deliverance from the ways of evil men (vv. 12–15)

A father instructed his son to listen to and seek wisdom (vv. 1–4). Fear and knowledge of God comes from the Lord, the source of wisdom (vv. 5–8). The Lord's wisdom provides moral discernment (vv. 9–11). Wisdom provides deliverance from evil men and their perverse ways (vv. 12–15).

I. Call to Listen to Wisdom (Prov. 2:1–4)

1 My son, if thou wilt receive my words, and hide my commandments with thee;

2 So that thou incline thine ear to wisdom, and apply thine heart to understanding;

3 Yea, if thou criest after knowledge and liftest up thy voice for understanding;

4 If thou seekest her as silver, and searchest for her as hid treasures.

Old Testament revelation took several forms. God revealed Himself through events like creation and the deliverance from Egypt. He revealed Himself through His dealings with people, through His covenant and His Commandments, and through the words and actions of the prophets. God also revealed Himself through the wisdom writings.

Wisdom in the Old Testament is insight from God for living life as it is intended to be lived. Human experience is prominent in the Wisdom Writings. Sometimes wisdom deals with the deep issues of the meaning of life and the purpose of human suffering. At other times, wisdom deals with everyday subjects like right and wrong, marriage, parenting, neighbors, work, wealth, speech, and so forth.

Although human experience is prominent, the wisdom of the Bible is not commonplace advice based on human observation and experience. Biblical wisdom is divine revelation. Wisdom comes from the Lord as surely as did the message of the prophets.

As we have already seen this quarter, the Wisdom Writings of the Old Testament are not all alike in form or approach. Ecclesiastes is the testimony of a man who sought to find meaning in life. Job is a drama of a good man's struggle to understand his suffering. Proverbs is a father's instructions, warnings, and insights to his son about how to live as God intends.

The basic teaching setting for the Book of Proverbs is the home, and the teacher is the father. The words "my son" occur many times (1:10, 15; 2:1; 3:1, 11, 21; 5:1). Proverbs 1:8 shows that the father was speaking for both parents. Of course, words of true wisdom are not only for the young but also for older people (1:5). Although the father spoke of "my words" and "my commandments" (2:1), he later made plain that God is the source of wisdom (2:6). Many scholars believe the wisdom that originated in the home was later also used by wise, fatherly teachers for young men.

Words like "wisdom," "understanding," and "knowledge" occur throughout the passage. This shows that the use of the intellect in an educational setting is basic; however, the education has a moral and a spiritual basis; and Hebrew wisdom always had a practical purpose that involved all kinds of people, not just the "intellectuals" of the day.

Notice the strong verbs that describe how people of faith are to respond to wisdom: "receive," "hide," "incline," "apply," "criest after," "liftest up," "kest," and "searchest for." The Hebrew word translated "hide" means to "store up." The same word appears in Psalm 119:11, "Thy word have I hid in mine heart, that I might not sin against thee." The words of wisdom were to be memorized and stored up for daily use in the same way as the words of the law.

The "ear" and "heart" are mentioned in verse 2. "Hear" reminds us of the words of Jesus after the parable of the soils: "He that hath ears to hear, let him hear" (Mark 4:9). The word "heart" in Hebrew usage meant more than emotion. It meant the mind and will, and it was often used of total commitment (Deut. 6:5).

The words "criest after" in verse 3 appeared also in Proverbs 1:20–21, where wisdom is personified and pictured as crying out for people to hear and heed her words. True wisdom is so right and reasonable that it is as though she calls out to be heard. Wisdom warns that many people will foolishly fail to listen (1:22–32). Wisdom, however, says, "But whoso hearkeneth unto me shall dwell safely, and shall be quiet from fear of evil" (Prov. 1:33). Proverbs 2:1–4 picks up this thought and reinforces it. Just as wisdom cries out for people, so should wise people cry out for wisdom. Although God and wisdom seek us, we must in turn respond.

Verse 4 stresses a search for wisdom, which is compared to silver or to hidden treasures. Wisdom has great value, just as the law was compared to gold and honey (Ps. 19:10). Jesus compared the kingdom of heaven to treasure that a man found in a field; he then sold everything he had to buy the land so he could have the precious treasure (Matt. 13:44).

II. Blessings of Listening to Wisdom (Prov. 2:5–15)

1. Fear and knowledge of God (vv. 5–8)

5 Then shalt thou understand the fear of the LORD, and find the knowledge of God.

6 For the LORD giveth wisdom: out of his mouth cometh knowledge and understanding.

7 He layeth up sound wisdom for the righteous: he is a buckler to them that walk uprightly.

8 He keepeth the paths of judgment, and preserveth the way of his saints.

Verses 1–4 is not a complete sentence. Notice "if" in verses 1,3–4. Verses 1–4 state certain conditions that, if met, will produce certain results. The word "then" in verse 5 begins the list of results or blessings that result from listening to wisdom. The basic double blessing of verse 5 is the fear and knowledge of God. To put it another way, when one seeks wisdom, the person fears and knows God. Knowledge of God in the Bible includes more than knowing facts about God; its basic meaning is personal knowledge of God. Thus, this refers to the intimacy of a personal relationship with God.

How does knowing God fit with fearing God? They are inseparable in the life of true faith. The key verse in Proverbs is 1:7, "The fear of the LORD is the beginning of knowledge." Our personal relationship with God is never "buddy-buddy." God remains the infinite God, whose ways are always beyond our understanding (Isa. 55:8–9) and in whose holy presence we become aware of our own unworthiness, sin, and mortality (Isa. 6:1–8). When God made the covenant with Israel at Mount Sinai, He impressed them with His holiness and power (Exod. 19). Hebrews 12:18–24 contrasts coming to Mount Sinai and coming to Mount Zion (Old Testament and New Testament revelation). Although the New Covenant stresses the grace and love of God, we are still reminded that "our God is a consuming fire" (Heb. 12:29).

Verses 7–8 stress how God and His wisdom preserve those who live by the righteous standards of God. The word "buckler" means "shield." "Keepeth" has the idea of watching or guarding. "Preserveth" is the same word used in Psalm 121, in which the psalmist testifies of the help found in looking to God. God is ever alert to keep His people: "The LORD shall preserve thee from all evil: he shall preserve thy soul" (Ps. 121:7).

This is the doctrine of the perseverance of the saints, which is more aptly called the *preservation* of the saints. God always has a stronger hold on us than we do on Him, and nothing can break that hold (John 10:27–29). This trust is expressed in Jude 24: "Now unto him that is able to keep you from falling, and to present you faultless before the presence of his glory with exceeding joy."

2. Moral discernment (vv. 9–11)

9 Then shalt thou understand righteousness, and judgment, and equity; yea, every good path.

10 When wisdom entereth into thine heart, and knowledge is pleasant unto thy soul;

11 Discretion shall preserve thee, understanding shall keep thee.

In some ways, verses 9–11 elaborate on verses 7–8. Those who seek wisdom find a new understanding of righteousness, justice, integrity, and every good way of living. This understanding includes strength to do right and joy in doing right. Doing right becomes pleasant. A basic assumption of biblical wisdom is that God's wisdom presents the only right and reasonable way to live. People find new insight, strength, and joy when they live according to the plan of their Creator.

A key idea in verses 9–11 is that wisdom provides moral discernment. Wisdom enables people to distinguish good from evil. Evil people (as we shall see in vv. 12–15) confuse good and evil. Isaiah 5:20 warned, "Woe unto them that call evil good, and good evil; that put darkness for light, and light for darkness; that put bitter for sweet, and sweet for bitter!" Hebrews 5:13–14 contrasts the moral discernment of mature and immature believers. The immature are "unskillful in the word of righteousness." The mature "have their senses exercised to discern both good and evil." In an age of moral confusion, we need this divine wisdom.

3. Deliverance from the ways of evil men (vv. 12–15)

12 To deliver thee from the way of the evil man, from the man that speaketh froward things;

13 Who leave the paths of uprightness, to walk in the ways of darkness;

14 Who rejoice to do evil, and delight in the frowardness of the wicked;

15 Whose ways are crooked, and they froward in their paths.

Do you remember how you felt when your child went away from home to college or, if you are younger, when your child entered junior high or high school? Godly parents do their best to teach their children how to do what is right. They know that as the children mature, they will increasingly be subjected to people who live by totally different standards. Some of these folks will seek to seduce the young people to follow them in their evil ways. Verses 12–15 promise that true wisdom will deliver youth and adults from giving in to the temptations offered by evil men. (Evil women are mentioned in vv. 16–19.)

The evil man is described in verses 12–15. His words as well as his actions are perverse. Evil men turn from the way of uprightness to the way of sin and darkness. Their evil ways are their source of pleasure. This is in contrast to the righteous, who rejoice in goodness (v. 10). Paul, a righteous man, wrote that the person who seeks sinful pleasures is dead, even while living (1 Tim. 5:6).

The word "froward" means "perverse" or "devious." In other words, the evil man is not only perverse himself but uses devious ways to lure others into the way of evil. An example of this is given in Proverbs 1:10–19. The father warned his son not to consent to the enticement of those who would involve him in crime in order to get money. Proverbs 5 warns against the sinful woman who seeks to seduce young men.

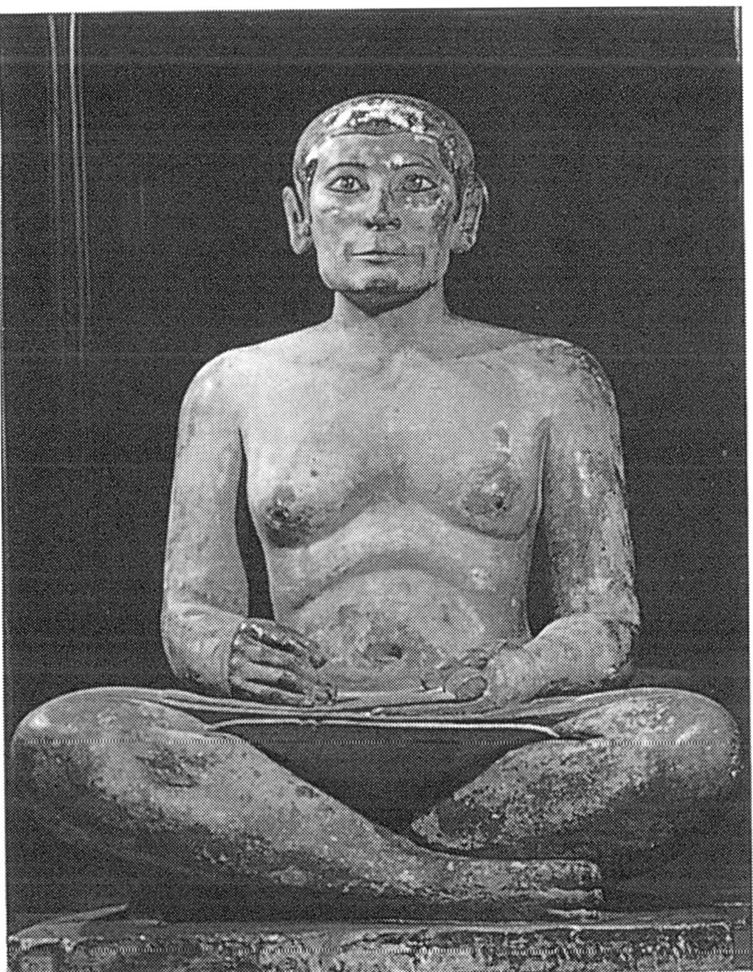

Wisdom was important in Egypt and in other ancient cultures. (Source: Holman Pictorial Collection of Biblical Antiquities, Holman Bible Publishers, Nashville, TN [Louvre, Paris]).

APPLYING THE TRUTH

1. Conveying knowledge. Today we focus on teaching—conveying truth to a succeeding generation. Engraved on the stone façade of the university's central administration building where I attended were these words: "The purveyors of knowledge are as important as the discoverers of knowledge." Every generation is but one generation away from total spiritual ignorance. Truth must be transferred!

2. The value of teaching. Robert Millikan, a professor of physics, once heard an employee in his household answer the telephone like this: "Yes, this is the residence of Dr. Millikan, but he's not the kind of doctor who does anybody any good." But teachers do an immense amount of good—or ill!

3. Ignorance and excitement. The comic strip philosopher Hagar once said to his son about learning: "Remember, Son: Ignorance is the mother of excitement." The problem is that ignorance (and sometimes, to use Peter's phrase, "willful ignorance!") always causes excitement of the wrong sort, and more than we planned for!

4. Daily in the Word. Billy Graham said it has been his personal goal for many years to read five of the Psalms every day, along with one chapter of the Book of Proverbs—making it possible to read through both books every month.

5. Parents as teachers. Note that throughout the Book of Proverbs, the emphasis (though not the sole emphasis) is upon the father teaching his children. That is a consistent biblical emphasis. Remember Paul's injunction: "Ye fathers, provoke not your children to wrath: but bring them up in the nurture and admonition of the Lord" (Eph. 6:4; see also Col. 3:21). What three truths did your father or mother teach you (by precept and practice) that have blessed your life? What answer will your child or children give to that question about you?

6. Spiritual mentors. My father was killed when I was an infant, and my surrogate father was not a Christian, though he became one after I was grown. Consider these two very important influences on my life: (a) Even though my surrogate father was not a Christian man, he taught me many valuable lessons about life, and I am in his debt forever because of that. (b) When I was converted at age seventeen, a man in our church took time to disciple me—to teach me personally about the things of Christ. He had been my Sunday school teacher for two years before I was saved, yet he told me, upon my conversion, that he never realized he was "getting through" to me when he taught. Actually, I had always admired him greatly and listened intently to everything he said. He was, and will always be, my most substantive spiritual mentor. The point? Somebody's listening even though they might not be acting like it!

7. To be a teacher. When one of my grandsons was converted, at age seven, his father asked him what he wanted to be when he grew up. The boy said, to a shocked and humbled father: "I want to teach tenth and eleventh grade boys in Sunday school just like you do!" He could have said he wanted to be a successful CPA, an honor graduate from a major university, an excellent athlete, a deacon, a building committee member, or a member of the pastor-search committee of a large church—all of which his dad was at the time—but he said he wanted to teach others about God! Is there a nobler ambition in the universe?

- *Main Idea:* Listening to wisdom provides great blessings.
- *Suggested Teaching Aim:* To lead adults to describe three blessings of listening to wisdom

A TEACHING OUTLINE

1. Use a graffiti wall to introduce the Bible study.
2. Use a lesson outline poster to guide the search for biblical truth.
3. Use group discussion to help members examine the biblical text.
4. Use small groups to involve members.
5. Use recall and group discussion to give the truth a personal focus.

Introduce the Bible Study

On a chalkboard or a large sheet of paper, write three or four proverbs such as those mentioned in "Studying the Bible." As members enter, ask them each to write a different proverb. Read the proverbs. Ask: How much wisdom do proverbs contain? Why do you think these statements became proverbs? Point out the new unit on the quarter poster, "Proverbs for Living a Disciplined Life." Explain that today we begin a new unit that will help us understand the divine wisdom of the biblical proverbs.

Search for Biblical Truth

Make a lesson outline poster by copying the outline in "Outline and Summary" on a large sheet of paper. Cover all the points until you are ready to teach them.

Uncover the first point, "I. Call to Listen to Wisdom (Prov. 2:1–4)." On a chalkboard or a large sheet of paper write:

How Has God Revealed Himself?

- Through events like creation and deliverance from Egypt.
- Through His dealings with people.
- Through His covenant and His Commandments.
- Through the words and actions of the prophets.
- Through the wisdom writings.

IN ADVANCE, write this definition on a large sheet of paper: "Wisdom in the Old Testament is insight from God for living life as it is intended to be lived." Read this definition. Ask members to look at 2:1–4 and answer:

Who is speaking? *A father*

To whom is he speaking? *His son*

Where is the basic setting for Proverbs? *The home*

Ask members to find the strong verbs in 2:1–4. Use "Studying the Bible" to explain the significance of these verbs.

Uncover the second point on the outline, "II. Blessings of Listening to Wisdom (Prov. 2:5–15)" as well as the three subpoints. Suggest that the text suggests three blessings. If your class works well in groups, form three groups (a group can be one or more persons), and assign each group one of the blessings. Ask each group to do the following: (1) read the Scripture; (2) summarize the Bible's teaching about the blessing; and (3) suggest how these verses would apply to believers today.

Allow about six to eight minutes for study and then call for reports. If you prefer, you can work together as a class instead of dividing into groups. If you choose that approach, uncover the blessings in the subpoints one at a time.

Give the Truth a Personal Focus

Ask members to suggest areas in which each of these blessings is (1) absent, and (2) present in today's society. Ask: What difference would it make if people today listened to wisdom in these three areas? What difference would it have made in your life this past week? What difference would it make this coming week? Close in prayer that all present will hear and obey God's wisdom.

Trust God

Basic Passage: Proverbs 3:1–20
Focal Passages: Proverbs 3:1–8, 11–15

Proverbs 3:5–6 is among the most famous passages in the book. These are favorite memory verses. When we trust God completely, He promises to direct us in the ways we should go. Verses 5–6 is one of six expressions of a life of trust in Proverbs 3:1–12. Each includes a promised reward. Proverbs 3:13–20 praises wisdom as more valuable than gold.

Study Aim: *To list some ways that wisdom expresses itself in a life of trust in God*

STUDYING THE BIBLE

OUTLINE AND SUMMARY

I. A Life of Trust (Prov. 3:1–12)
- **1. Remembering God's Commandments (vv. 1–2)**
- **2. Kind and trustworthy (vv. 3–4)**
- **3. Total reliance on God (vv. 5–6)**
- **4. Reverent trust, not sinful pride (vv. 7–8)**
- **5. Worshiping God through giving (vv. 9–10)**
- **6. Accepting the Lord's discipline (vv. 11–12)**

II. Praise of Wisdom (Prov. 3:13–20)
- **1. More valuable than gold (vv. 13–15)**
- **2. Life and peace (vv. 16–18)**
- **3. Wisdom in creation (vv. 19–20)**

Remembering God's Commandments brings life and peace (vv. 1–2). Being kind and trustworthy pleases God and others (vv. 3–4). God guides those who totally rely on Him (vv. 5–6). Replacing sinful pride with reverent trust produces health and strength (vv. 7–8). God blesses those who honor Him by giving their best (vv. 9–10). God's discipline shows His fatherly love (vv. 11–12). Those who find wisdom discover greater wealth than gold (vv. 13–15). Wisdom blesses with life and peace (3:16–18). God used wisdom in creation (vv. 19–20).

I. A Life of Trust (Prov. 3:1–12)

1. Remembering God's Commandments (vv. 1–2)

1 My son, forget not my law; but let thine heart keep my commandments;

2 For the length of days, and long life, and peace, shall they add to thee.

Chapter 3 begins much like chapter 2. A father speaks to his son about his commandments. Although the father said "my commandments," he was communicating God's Commandments (see Deut. 4:9; 6:6–7). Proverbs 2:1 emphasizes hearing and hiding while 3:1 stresses remembering and keeping. The Books of Proverbs and Deuteronomy have many things in common. One is the stress on remembering (Deut. 8:11), not remembering (Deut. 8:18).

Long life is presented in the Old Testament as a blessing of faith and obedience. For example, the promised blessing for honoring one's parents is long life (Exod. 20:12; Deut. 5:16). The word "peace" means "wholeness, harmony." In other words, the person who remembers God's Commandments is promised a rich, full life. This is a basic assumption of biblical wisdom. It enables people to live as their Creator intended.

2. Kind and trustworthy (vv. 3–4)

> **3 Let not mercy and truth forsake thee: bind them about thy neck; write them upon the table of thine heart:**
>
> **4 So shalt thou find favour and good understanding in the sight of God and man.**

The Hebrew words translated "mercy" and "truth" are key Old Testament terms. Exodus 34:6–7 stresses that God is "abundant in goodness and truth." "Mercy" or "goodness" is a word used to describe the covenant of God. "Truth" is "trustworthiness" or "faithfulness." The same words are also used to describe God's people. Jacob used these words of Joseph in Genesis 47:29. The two Israelite spies, whom Rahab hid, promised her, "We will deal kindly and truly with thee" (Josh. 2:14).

Verse 3 warns against letting these things slip away. Instead, people of faith should bind them about their necks and write them on their hearts. The same language was used in Deuteronomy 6:6–7. These qualities must be so integrated into our thoughts and attitudes that they are reflected in our words and deeds.

Those who prove to be kind and trustworthy are highly esteemed by both God and other people. Do you not treasure a person who treats you kindly and who deals with you in a trustworthy way?

3. Total reliance on God (vv. 5–6)

> **5 Trust in the LORD with all thine heart; and lean not unto thine own understanding.**
>
> **6 In all thy ways acknowledge him, and he shall direct thy paths.**

These are the verses in Proverbs 3 that many of us have memorized. These are good verses to say at the beginning of each new day and as you face each decision. The word translated "trust" means to "rely on," to "have confidence in." It is related in meaning to the word "lean." Rather than relying or leaning on ourselves and our limited understanding, we should rely on the Lord. The words "with all thine heart" are found more than once in the Old Testament. For example, the Lord promised the people going into exile, "Ye shall seek me, and find me, when ye shall search for me with all your heart" (Jer. 29:13). The phrase refers to total reliance on the Lord. The same idea is expressed in different words in the first line of verse 6. Acknowledging the Lord in all our ways means making Him Lord of every aspect of our lives and seeking His direction in every way we take.

The promise is: "He shall direct thy paths." This has the idea of making our paths straight. This doesn't mean that God promises to make the road of life smooth for people of faith. It means that God shows us what road to take and goes with us on the road. This promise applies to life as a whole and to each of life's decisions. As we live our faith day by day, people who totally rely on God can be assured that He is guiding us. As we face a difficult decision, He will show us which fork in the road to take.

Paul wrote, "We walk by faith, not by sight" (2 Cor. 5:7). Hebrews 11 describes the heroes of faith. Verse 1 reminds us that believing is seeing, not seeing is believing. Verse 8 says that Abraham headed out into the unknown by faith in God. God did not supply Abraham with a marked road map. Abraham did not even know where God was leading him until he got there. God shines enough light on our paths to enable us to take the next step. Then we trust that He will shine the light on the next step.

4. Reverent trust, not sinful pride (vv. 7–8)

7 Be not wise in thine own eyes: fear the Lord, and depart from evil.

8 It shall be health to thy navel, and marrow to thy bones.

The first clause in verse 7 repeats the warning in the last line of verse 5. Those who rely on their own understanding are people who regard their own wisdom too highly. Usually, they are so self-confident that they go through life without seeking God's direction and wisdom. This is a basic human sin because it replaces God with ourselves. The beginning of true wisdom is to fear the Lord (Prov. 1:7). This kind of reverent trust in God is incompatible with sinful pride and other human sins.

Those who replace sinful pride with reverent trust are promised health and strength. The "navel" represented the beginning of life after birth. "Bones" referred to health and well-being. "Marrow" meant healthy bones. Translators use words like "health," "strength," and "refreshment" to describe the well-being that results from reverent trust. This is another way of saying that it leads us to live as God intended and to experience the good life He wants us to have. Based on the total biblical revelation, we know that this is not an unqualified promise of good health to people of faith. Job's experience shows that. Paul wrote that faith does not exempt believers from sickness, aging, and mortality; however, he wrote, "Though our outward man perish, yet the inward man is renewed day by day" (2 Cor. 4:16).

5. Worshiping God through giving (vv. 9–10)

People of faith honor and worship God through giving back to Him from the material things with which He has blessed them (v. 9). Generous giving brings blessings in turn to those who give (v. 10).

6. Accepting the Lord's discipline (vv. 11–12)

11 My son, despise not the chastening of the LORD; neither be weary of his correction:

12 For whom the LORD loveth he correcteth; even as a father the son in whom he delighteth.

The word translated "chastening" is often translated "instruction." This is the word, for example, in Proverbs 4:1: "Hear, ye children, the instruction of a father." The word sometimes has the idea of punishment in it, but it also has the idea of God using life as a means of instructing His children. The issue, of course, is this: Does the Old Testament teach that trouble is always punishment for sin, and prosperity is reward for godly living? Some verses in Proverbs 3 promise long life (v. 2), good health (v. 8), and prosperity (v. 10) to good people. From our study of Job, we remember that Job's three friends believed that trouble and sickness are punishment for sin. The conclusion of the Book of Job (42:1–17) and the New Testament show that although this is sometimes true (John 5:14), it is not always true (John 9:1–3).

Some Bible students claim that Proverbs 3:11–12 teaches the same thing that Job's three friends believed. However, these verses teach a larger lesson. Life has its troubles and trials. People of faith experience these as do unbelievers. Some of these may be punishments from God, but troubles are often the means whereby a loving Father seeks to instruct His children. Most of us learn more about the really important things in the school of life than we do in any other school. Paul, for example, wrote that he was better equipped to comfort others by having passed through the school of suffering (2 Cor. 1:3–4).

Proverbs 3:11 tells us not to refuse to learn from the lessons of divine discipline. Verse 12 assures us that such troubles are a sign of the Father's love just as an earthly father's discipline is done in love. Hebrews 12:5–11 quotes and applies this passage. God in love teaches us many lessons in the sometimes painful school of life. Hebrews 12:11 honestly acknowledges that such discipline is often painful at the time; only in retrospect are we able to see the hand of a loving Father.

II. Praise of Wisdom (Prov. 3:13–20)

1. More valuable than gold (vv. 13–15)

13 Happy is the man that findeth wisdom, and the man that getteth understanding.

14 For the merchandise of it is better than the merchandise of silver, and the gain thereof than fine gold.

15 She is more precious than rubies; and all the things thou canst desire are not to be compared unto her.

The word translated "happy" in verse 13 and in many other Old Testament passages (Prov. 14:21; 16:20) is translated "blessed" in Psalm 1:1. The word "merchandise" has the meaning "profit." There is no happiness to compare with the happiness of the person who finds wisdom. Likewise, nothing is so valuable or profitable as finding wisdom. (Compare Prov. 2:4; 8:11, 19.)

The latter point is illustrated and reinforced by four comparisons. Finding wisdom is more profitable than silver, gold, and rubies, or all the things that a person desires. The silver and gold comparisons remind us of Jesus' parable of the hidden treasure (Matt. 13:44). The rubies remind us of Jesus' parable of the pearl of great price (Matt. 13:45–46). The fourth comparison reminds us of the words of Paul in Philippians 3:7–8.

2. Life and peace (vv. 16–18)

Wisdom is pictured with long life in one hand and riches and honor in the other (v. 16). Her ways are pleasant ways of peace (v. 17). She is a tree of life to those happy ones who lay hold on her (v. 18).

3. Wisdom in creation (vv. 19–20)

Wisdom is a guiding principle used by God in creating and sustaining the universe.

APPLYING THE BIBLE

1. Trust and obey. Our study today is about trusting God. When I first came to Christ as a seventeen-year-old, one of the first songs of faith I learned was "Trust and Obey." The words of that hymn encouraged me at every crisis of faith—which began, of course, immediately. I began to do two things: trust and obey. If we trust and do not obey, we're in trouble; and if we obey and do not trust, we're in trouble! Remember: in biblical thought, trusting God actually entailed obeying God; one could not do one without the other. The two can actually be labeled as one act, as in "trust/obey" or "obey/trust." How is God, today, asking you to trust/obey?

2. No end. Two third-grade boys were walking home from school one afternoon. One exclaimed to the other, "First grade, second grade, third grade! Where's it all going to end?" The life of faith/obedience ("trust/obey") never ends. Who ever graduated from that school?

3. In God we trust. Recent studies indicate that the level of trust by Americans in our institutions—the government, the military, the various professions, even the church—has fallen to an all-time low. Many argue that this lack of trust has been earned by leaders of those institutions. Have you thought recently how gloriously wonderful it is never to have to be afraid that God is going to let us down? G. K. Chesterton once observed that trust in humankind was a recent—and very dangerous—heresy. He said no biblical writer would have ever thought of doing such a thing. On the other hand, there is a striking promise in the Bible: "Whosoever believeth on him shall not be ashamed" (Rom. 10:11). That refers to trust in God, not trust in other persons.

4. High stupidity. A cleaning maid, worn and weary after a long day's work on a steamy summer day, said to her helper, "Wow, is it ever hot!" Her comrade in moppery said, "Yeah, and the stupidity is high, too, ain't it?" Unless a leader, or an institution, walks in divine wisdom, "the stupidity" will be very high.

5. God is wiser than I. A professor at a major university sat in my office yesterday. I had had the privilege, last week, of leading him to Christ. He made a profession of faith Sunday and will be baptized Sunday after next. During our conversation, in which he spoke of what he had previously thought about God, he said, "Actually, I had created a god whom I liked very much, and whom I could easily manipulate. I said things like, 'My god wouldn't do this or that,' or 'My god would handle the matter this way, or that way.' I now know that my god has miserably failed me." I said to him, "If you thought like that, you were, of course, your own god; it wasn't God, but yourself that you trusted. No wonder your god failed!" He agreed, and expressed great gratitude to know a God who was bigger—and wiser—than himself.

6. "Nowhere else to go." Abraham Lincoln's religious pilgrimage has been the subject of great debate, but there can be no doubt that he came to a full-fledged commitment to Christ as his own personal Savior. Even before he became fully committed to Christ, however, he often spoke of his total dependence on God. Characteristic of such trust is his statement: "I have been driven many times upon my knees by the overwhelming conviction that I had nowhere else to go. My own wisdom, and that of all about me, seemed insufficient for that day."[1]

TEACHING THE BIBLE

- *Main Idea:* A life built on trust in God will demonstrate that trust by the way it is lived.
- *Suggested Teaching Aim:* To lead adults to describe elements of a life built on trust in God

A TEACHING OUTLINE

1. Use a hymn to introduce the Bible study.

2. Use a lesson outline poster to guide the search for biblical truth.

3. Consider using small groups to involve members.

4. Use lecture and group discussion.

5. Use personal examination to give the truth a personal focus.

Introduce the Bible Study

Sing or read the words to "Trust and Obey." Read the "Main Idea" and suggest that this lesson will help members describe elements of a life built on trust in God.

Search for Biblical Truth

IN ADVANCE, make a lesson outline poster in the shape of a circle divided into six pie-shaped wedges. Place the heading on the focal wall:

A Life of Trust (Prov. 3:1–12)

1. Remembering God's Commandments (3:1–2)
2. Kind and trustworthy (3:3–4)
3. Total reliance on God (3:5–6)
4. Reverent trust, not sinful pride (3:7–8)
5. Worshiping God through giving (3:9–10)
6. Accepting the Lord's discipline (3:11–12)

Using the material in "Studying the Bible," develop a lecture describing a life of trust in God. (Or, if your class works well in small groups of one or more, form six groups and give each of them one of the six outline points. Ask each group to [1] describe the action; [2] explain the words; [3] state the promise; and [4] relate the action to their daily lives.)

IN ADVANCE, enlist someone to read the Scripture when you call for it. Place the first point on the outline beneath the title and call for the reader to read 3:1–2. Use the four steps described above for the small groups and present that material in a lecture. If you have a large chalkboard, you could make a chart with the four steps down the side and the six actions listed in six parallel columns.

DISCUSS: How do you explain the promise of "long life" in the case of those righteous persons whose lives are cut short? Does our study from Job speak to this?

Place the second point on the outline and call for the reader to read 3:3–4. Using the four steps described above, present a brief lecture.

DISCUSS: Why do you treasure a person who treats you kindly and who deals with you in a trustworthy way?

IN ADVANCE, make a poster with the words of 3:5–6 on it and place the poster on the wall. Place the third point on the outline and call for the reader to read 3:5–6. Using the four steps described above, present a brief lecture.

DISCUSS: How has God fulfilled this promise in your life?

Place the fourth point on the outline and call for the reader to read 3:7–8. Using the four steps described above, present a brief lecture.

DISCUSS: If this promise is true, why do devout believers get sick?

Place the fifth point on the outline and call for the reader to read 3:9–10. Since these verses are outside the focal passage, just mention giving as a part of trusting and move to the next point.

Place the sixth point on the outline and call for the reader to read 3:11–12. Using the four steps described above, present a brief lecture.

DISCUSS: How can we determine if our trouble is punishment for our sins and our prosperity a reward for our godly living?

Call for the reader to read 3:13–15. Using "Studying the Bible," point out the four comparisons that show the value of finding wisdom.

Give the Truth a Personal Focus

Ask members to examine the six elements of a life built on trust in God. Distribute paper and pencils. Ask them to choose one area in which they are weak and to write one thing they will do to improve in that area this week.

---

1. William J. Johnson, *Abraham Lincoln: The Christian* (Nashville: Abingdon, 1913), 116.

JULY

19

1998

Be a Good Neighbor

Basic Passages: Proverbs 3:27–35; 14:21
Focal Passages: Proverbs 3:27–35; 14:21

"Who is my neighbour?" Luke 10:29 tells how a man asked Jesus this question. The man was trying to limit the definition of "neighbor." Jesus told a story showing that all people are our neighbors. The Old Testament word for "neighbor" means "friend," "companion," or "fellow"; but its use in the Old Testament supports the broader definition of Jesus. This will be apparent in this study of "neighbor" in Proverbs.

➧ **Study Aim:** *To describe what good neighbors do and what they do not do*

STUDYING THE BIBLE

OUTLINE AND SUMMARY

I. Contrasting Ways to Treat Neighbors (Prov. 14:21)

II. How to Be a Good Neighbor (Prov. 3:27–30)

1. What to do (3:27–28)

2. What not to do (3:29–30)

III. Why Not to Envy the Wicked (Prov. 3:31–35)

1. Do not envy wicked oppressors (3:31)

2. God punishes sinners, but rewards the righteous (3:32–35)

Despising a neighbor is a sin, but happy is the person who shows mercy on the poor (14:21). Don't withhold or postpone doing good for a neighbor (3:27–28). Don't scheme against or fight with a neighbor (3:29–30). Don't envy or mimic the wicked (3:31). The wicked stand under God's judgment, but God bestows grace and blessings on the humble (3:32–35).

I. Contrasting Ways to Treat Neighbors (Prov. 14:21)

21 He that despiseth his neighbour sinneth: but he that hath mercy on the poor, happy is he.

Proverbs 14:21 is one of many scattered verses in Proverbs that mentions "neighbor." The English word appears nineteen times in the King James Version. These references include the ones in Proverbs 3:28–29. One of the others is Proverbs 14:20, which sets the stage for verse 21. Verse 20 is a sad commentary on human nature: "The poor is hated even of his own neighbour: but the rich hath many friends." This is not the action of a good neighbor—to look down on the poor while befriending the rich.

Verse 21 makes clear that the person who despises his neighbor is guilty of sin; whereas, the person who shows mercy on the poor is happy and blessed. Doing good for the poor is a strong theme in the Old Testament. Withholding good from the poor is sin (Exod. 23:6, 11; Deut. 15:7–10; 24:10–22).

Verse 22 gives this additional explanation: "Do they not err that devise evil? but mercy and truth shall be to them that devise good." Notice that the words "mercy and truth" in verse 22 are the same words in Proverbs 3:3. As we noted in commenting on that verse, lovingkindness and trustworthiness are attributes of God that are to be reflected in the lives of His people.

II. How to Be a Good Neighbor (Prov. 3:27–30)

1. What to do (3:27–28)

27 Withhold not good from them to whom it is due, when it is in the power of thine hand to do it.

28 Say not unto thy neighbour, Go, and come again, and to morrow I will give; when thou hast it by thee.

Proverbs 14:21 presents two striking contrasts in ways to treat poor neighbors. Despising and showing mercy are at opposite extremes. Many people's actions fall somewhere between these extremes. Many, for example, ignore their poor neighbors. Proverbs 3:27–28 shows that withholding good from others doesn't inflict direct injury on them, but it is also sinful because it fails to meet their needs. Jesus stressed this point by picturing the priest and Levite passing by the injured man. They had not robbed and beaten him, but they left him to die (Luke 10:30–32).

Proverbs 3:27–28 describe sins of omission. James 4:17 says, "To him that knoweth to do good, and doeth it not, to him it is sin." Verse 27 warns against failing to do good when we have the power to do it. Verse 28 warns against postponing the good until tomorrow.

What is "good," and who are "them to whom it is due"? The Old Testament offers several possibilities. The principle would apply to workers who were due to be paid by their employer. It would apply to the poor who were asking for help, perhaps for permission to glean in the fields of a rich farmer. It would apply to the oppressed who asked the elders for justice. As far as the Old Testament law was concerned, each of these groups was asking no more than it was their right to ask.

The Old Testament also commanded that these groups be helped promptly. The poor lived from day to day. Many were day laborers. Their wages were due on the day they worked (Lev. 19:13). Failing to pay workers was a sin for which employers must answer God (James 5:4). Pledges, often the cloaks that served at night as blankets, taken from the poor were to be returned by sunset (Deut. 24:10–13). Other kinds of help and justice were not to be postponed.

Postponing help is usually just an excuse. The excuse-maker often has the resources at the time he makes the excuse. He just wants to avoid doing good. Proverbs 3:28 has much in common with James 2:15–16: "If a brother or sister be naked, and destitute of daily food, and one of you say unto them, Depart in peace, be ye warmed and filled; notwithstanding ye give them not those things which are needful to the body; what doth it profit?"

If verses 27–28 were stated positively, they would admonish us to do good to others insofar as we were able and to do good promptly. The New Testament word for "love" is *agape*. The basic meaning of the word is to do good to the other person. Jesus gave a definition of a good neighbor in Luke 10:30–37. The Samaritan could have followed the example of the priest and Levite and passed by on the other side. He had the resources to help, but the other two also probably had the necessary resources to help. The difference was that he acted to do good to the injured man and to do it right away. To have postponed helping the man probably would have led to his death. The Samaritan risked his life, took the time, did the first aid, hauled the injured man, and paid for his lodging and care. This is a good neighbor. We should remember, too, that the "neighbor" in this case was no doubt a total stranger, very likely even a man of another ethnic group.

2. What not to do (3:29–30)

> **29 Devise not evil against thy neighbour, seeing he dwelleth securely by thee.**
>
> **30 Strive not with a man without cause, if he have done thee no harm.**

Verses 27–28 describe sins of omission against one's neighbor. Verses 29–30 describe active sins of commission. Verse 29 warns against plotting evil or scheming against one's neighbor. This sin is made all the worse because the neighbor trusts the schemer. Verse 30 warns against arguing and fighting with a neighbor, especially if the neighbor has done no harm.

The biblical account of the sad fate of Naboth illustrates an extreme example of devising evil against a trusting neighbor (1 Kings 21:1–14). Naboth was literally the neighbor of King Ahab. How would you like to live next door to a couple like Ahab and Jezebel? Naboth had every reason to trust that he was safe. After all, his neighbor was none other than the king. He also felt safe because he was respected in the community and because it was a society governed by the laws of God's justice. However, evil scheming of a ruthless neighbor showed how misplaced was Naboth's trust.

Have you ever known of neighbors who waged a kind of war against one another for years? Such neighbors go out of their way to make life miserable for their hated neighbor. Often the cause of the dispute has been all but forgotten over the years. Since the Bible defines "neighbor" as more than the person next door, the application of verse 30 is as broad as humanity.

Writing to Christians, Paul said, "If it be possible, as much as lieth in you, live peaceably with all men" (Rom. 12:18). This command is found in a passage about Christians being mistreated and persecuted. Following the teachings and example of Jesus, Paul, therefore, wrote, "Be not overcome of evil, but overcome evil with good" (Rom. 12:21). In other words, Christians need to see Proverbs 3:30 from the New Testament perspective. Even if our neighbor has done us harm and we feel we have cause to retaliate, Jesus and Paul caution us against becoming no better than those who hurt us. Instead, we should seek to be peacemakers.

III. Why Not to Envy the Wicked (Prov. 3:31–35)

1. Do not envy wicked oppressors (3:31)

31 Envy thou not the oppressor, and choose none of his ways.

Sometimes good people wonder if their goodness is worth the effort. They strive to avoid the sins described in verses 27–30, in other words, to be a good neighbor. Yet they see other people who commit these and other sins; and many of these violent, sinful people seem to be doing better than they themselves are.

Psalm 73 is the classic biblical passage on envying the wicked. The psalmist testified how he had almost slipped because he began to envy the wicked (vv. 1–3). The wicked seemed to prosper in life and to die painless deaths even though they mocked God by word and deed (vv. 4–10). The psalmist asked whether God was aware of this (vv. 11–14). He gained new insight in God's sanctuary (vv. 15–17). Then he saw that the wicked were living on a slippery slope to doom (vv. 18–20). As he berated himself for his own foolish thoughts, the psalmist got a new vision of his own rich fellowship with the Lord, the greatest of all treasures (vv. 21–28).

Proverbs 31–35 reaches similar conclusions. After the warning of verse 31, verses 32–35 show the striking contrast in God's treatment of the righteous and the wicked.

2. God punishes sinners, but rewards the righteous (3:32–35)

32 For the froward is abomination to the LORD: but his secret is with the righteous.

33 The curse of the LORD is in the house of the wicked: but he blesseth the habitation of the just.

34 Surely he scorneth the scorners: but he giveth grace unto the lowly.

35 The wise shall inherit glory: but shame shall be the promotion of fools.

These verses explain why the righteous should not envy or mimic the wicked. The four verses present four striking contrasts between God's treatment of the wicked and the righteous. Four different pairs of words are used to describe good and evil people. Four contrasting fates are presented for each.

The "froward," or "perverse," are contrasted with the righteous. The perverse are people whose lives are twisted by sin. They are an abomination to the Lord. By contrast, God's "secret" or "confidence" is with the righteous. The word translated "secret" connotes fellowship, status, and unity. God's people have such a relationship with God.

God's curse rests on the house of the wicked, but His blessing rests on the house of the just. This may not be apparent except to eyes of faith. The property of the wicked may be more valuable and beautiful in earthly measurements, but a divine curse hangs over it. By the same token, the upright person may live in a modest house; but God's favor rests on it.

The wicked often scorn others and even scorn God. Scorning is a mark of blind pride to one's own sins and to the value of others. People reap what they sow. The scorners will be scorned by God. The opposite of pride is humility. God gives grace to the humble. This is quoted in James 4:6 and 1 Peter 5:5.

Two favorite words in Proverbs are "wise" and "fool." The wise are people who live by God's wisdom; the fools are those who reject God's wisdom and live by their own ways. Each receives an inheritance. The inheritance of the wise is glory and honor, while fools receive only shame.

Wisdom Literature

The Books of Poetry are also called Books of Wisdom. Wisdom literature was an ancient literary form.

Sometimes the wisdom took the form of practical advice about everyday living, as in Proverbs. Sometimes wisdom literature wrestled with the ultimate questions of life, as in Job and Ecclesiastes.

Most of the psalms are songs of praise, confession, petition, and testimony rather than wisdom literature. The following, however, are wisdom psalms: 1, 37, 49, 73, 112, 127, 128, 133.

APPLYING THE BIBLE

1. Good Neighbors. F. D. Roosevelt, in 1933, led Congress to establish a Good Neighbor Policy with Latin American nations. The Book of Proverbs establishes, once and for all, a "Good Neighbor Policy" for all human beings. It must be obvious to the most cursory student of human history that we haven't done a very good job with neighboring! In fact, history is a demonstration of a wag's word: Proximity without community is calamity!

2. Everybody's friend. Sam Walter Foss wrote these familiar lines about being a neighbor:

Let me live in a house by the side of the road,
Where the race of men go by—
The men who are good and the men who are bad,
As good and as bad as I.
I would not sit in the scorner's seat,
Or hurl the cynic's ban;
Let me live in a house by the side of the road
And be a friend to man.

3. Fences. In his poem "The Mending Wall," Robert Frost states, "Good fences make good neighbors." But, often, fences are designed to keep others out of our lives, not to mark off legitimate boundaries. This tendency increases in a culture where people hardly know, or wish to know, their "neighbors." The poet Elizabeth Cutter wrote,

My friend and I have built a wall
Between us thick and wide:
The stones of it are laid in scorn
And plastered high with pride.

4. Love for neighbors. A man once said he believed in the Fatherhood of God, the brotherhood of man, and the neighborhood of Philadelphia. That is at least the beginnings of a good and healthy theology—and sociology!

5. The "biggest" half. Two neighbor boys were always fighting. One day one of their mothers, listening to another of their interminable arguments, cut an apple in two and said, "Now, you go right over there and give him the 'biggest' half!" The boy said, later, that he thought, "Yeah, I'll give him the 'biggest' half—right in the ear!" As he came to the fence between the yards, some bit of sanity flitted through his brain; he stuck the "biggest" half through the fence and said, "There, go and choke on it!" The two boys became friends for life, and neither ever forgot the gift of the "biggest" half.

6. The two great commandments of life. Jesus said, "Thou shalt love the Lord thy God with all thy heart, and with all they soul, and with all thy strength, and with all thy mind; And thy neighbour as thyself" (Luke 10:27). What evidence does your neighbor have that you love him?

7. True "neighborhoods." It is important for Christians to remember that our churches are "neighborhoods" too. See Psalm 133 about how important it is for "brethren to dwell together in unity." Shakespeare has a line about that: "We few, we happy few, we band of brothers" (*King Henry V,* 4.3.60). That is a beautiful description of God's ideal for His church!

8. With Nelson. Sir Robert Stopford, an English sailor, once wrote about a dangerous naval experiment in which the English navy chased to the West Indies a fleet nearly their double in number. After telling about the desperate situation and the terrible conditions, Stopford added, "We are half-starved, and otherwise inconvenienced by being so long out of port. But our reward is—we are with Nelson!"[1]

8. Neighborhood and brotherhood. Lyndon B. Johnson once said, "We live in a world that has narrowed into a neighborhood before it has broadened into a brotherhood." That describes too many churches! What can the members of your class do to create a stronger sense of "neighborhood" in your church?

TEACHING THE BIBLE

- *Main Idea:* Being a good neighbor pleases God.
- *Suggested Teaching Aim:* To lead adults to identify ways they can be good neighbors

A TEACHING OUTLINE

1. Use a life situation to introduce the Bible study.

2. Use charts and group discussion to guide the search for biblical truth.

3. Use personal examination to give the truth a personal focus.

Introduce the Bible Study

Read: "Bob was out visiting for his church on Thursday evening. He had an appointment at 7:30 P.M. with a prospective family who had just moved to town. They had attended Downtown Church for the last three Sundays, and Bob was certain they would join Downtown Church even though they had to pass Suburban Church on the way. He glanced at his watch. He was running late. If he went around by the regular route, he would be late. He could cut through the old part of town and make it. As he drove through the dark streets, he unconsciously locked the doors of the car. As he rounded a curve, his headlights picked up two men bending over a third man, who was lying on the sidewalk. When they saw his lights, the two men broke and ran, leaving the third man on the sidewalk. Bob hesitated for a moment, trying to decide what he should do, then he . . ."[2]

Ask several members to suggest what Bob did. Suggest that today's lesson gives them some principles for being good neighbors.

Search for Biblical Truth

IN ADVANCE, write each of the following Scripture references on a separate sheet of paper and post these around the room: Luke 10:25–37; James 4:17; 1 Kings 21:1–14; Romans 12:21.

On a chalkboard or a large sheet of paper, write these headings (members will add italicized phrases):

How to Be a Good Neighbor

Positive	Negative
1. *Show mercy.*	*Do not despise.*
2. *Do all you can to help quickly.*	*Do not withhold goods/services.*
3. *Do good.*	*Do not do evil.*
4. *Be agreeable.*	*Do not argue.*

Ask members to open their Bibles to Proverbs 14:21 and find one positive and one negative way to be a good neighbor. Write these on the above chart. Ask members to look around the room at the Scriptures and find one that illustrates someone who showed mercy (Luke 10:25–37). Ask members to develop a principle that expresses these teachings.

DISCUSS: Since many poor people have brought their poverty on themselves, Christians should not take their hard-earned resources to help them.

Ask members to look at 3:27–28 and find a negative way to be a good neighbor. Write that on the chart; also state it positively. Ask members to look around the room at the Scriptures and find one that encourages us to do good (James 4:17). Ask members to develop a principle that expresses this teaching.

DISCUSS: Do we ever have a responsibility to place ourselves at risk to help someone we don't know? Or someone we do know?

Ask members to look at 3:29–30 and find two negatively stated ways of being a good neighbor. Write them on the chart; also state them positively. Ask members to look around the room at the Scriptures and find one that illustrates how someone did harm to a neighbor (1 Kings 21:1–14) and one that describes how we should live with all people if possible (Rom. 12:18). Ask members to develop two principles that express this teaching.

DISCUSS: What do you do when you have just cause to argue with a neighbor?

Ask: Why do some people envy those who mistreat others? Ask members to look at 3:31–35. Write the chart below on a chalkboard. Ask half the class to find four descriptions of the wicked and what will happen to them, and ask the other half to find four descriptions of the righteous and what will happen to them.

Negative		Positive	
Person	**Promise**	**Person**	**Promise**
perverse	*abomination*	*righteous*	*confidence*
wicked	*curse*	*just*	*blessed*
scorners	*scorned*	*lowly*	*grace*
fools	*shame*	*wise*	*glory*

Give the Truth a Personal Focus

Read the four principles members developed earlier in which they summarized how to be a good neighbor. Ask, Based on these principles, how good a neighbor are you? Challenge members to apply these principles to their lives.

---

1. Quoted in Jamb Stewart, *Heralds of God* (London: Hodder & Stoughton, 1946), 144.
2. James E. Taulman, *Help! I Need an Idea* (Nashville: Broadman Press, 1987), 117–18.

Obey God's Law

Basic Passage: Proverbs 28:1–13
Focal Passages: Proverbs 28:4–10, 13

The divisions of our English Bibles are Law, History, Poetry (Wisdom), and Prophets. The Law records God's covenant with Israel and His Commandments. The Books of History tell how the people failed to obey God's laws. The Prophets record the words of God's preachers who admonished the people to obey God's laws. The Wisdom Books explain why obeying God's laws is the wise and prudent way to live.

Study Aim: *To explain why wise people obey God's law and foolish people don't*

STUDYING THE BIBLE

OUTLINE AND SUMMARY

I. Personal and Social Consequences of Sin (Prov. 28:1–3)

II. Wisdom to Know and Do What Is Right (Prov. 28:4–7)
  1. Moral conviction or confusion? (vv. 4–5)
  2. True wealth (v. 6)
  3. Family values (v. 7)

III. Sin and Retribution (Prov. 28:8–12)
  1. Losing unjust gains (v. 8)
  2. Unanswered prayers (v. 9)
  3. Caught in your own trap (v. 10)
  4. Folly of sin (vv. 11–12)

IV. Confession and Mercy (Prov. 28:13)

Sin has evil consequences on everyone from individuals to nations (vv. 1–3). God's law provides moral convictions, but forsaking the law leads to moral confusion (vv. 4–5). A poor upright man has more wealth than a perverse rich man (v. 6). A son who keeps the law honors his father, but a son who joins others in riotous living shames his father (v. 7). Those who get rich by exploiting the poor will lose their wealth to those who share generously with the poor (v. 8). The prayers of those who disobey God's law are an abomination to the Lord (v. 9). The evil person who digs a pit to trap the innocent righteous will fall into the pit he dug (v. 10). Sin is irrational because it blinds people to their real condition and spreads harm in all directions (vv. 11–12). No one can conceal his sins from God, but the sinner who confesses and forsakes his sins will receive divine mercy (v. 13).

I. Personal and Social Consequences of Sin (Prov. 28:1–3)

The wicked try to run away from a guilty conscience, but the righteous can face life unafraid (v. 1). The fate of a nation depends on the moral character of its people and leaders (v. 2). Oppression, whether by rich or poor, is destructive (v. 3).

II. Wisdom to Know and Do What Is Right (Prov. 28:4–7)

1. Moral conviction or confusion? (vv. 4–5)

4 They that forsake the law praise the wicked: but such as keep the law contend with them.

5 Evil men understand not judgment: but they that seek the LORD understand all things.

A person's attitude toward wicked people reveals a lot about the person. Some persons praise evil people. They make heroes of them and take them as examples of how to live. Other persons disagree completely with the way evil people live. They oppose the evil and, if need be, the evil people. Verse 4 says that people who praise the wicked have forsaken God's law. They have rejected God's Commandments as absolute standards for how to live. Those who are critical of evil and evil people are persons who know and accept God's Commandments as authoritative rules on how to live.

Many people in every age have denied that God's Commandments provide absolute moral principles by which to live. Today, we call this view "moral relativism." The view holds that right and wrong are matters of personal choice that vary from culture to culture, from person to person, or even from situation to situation. The Ten Commandments are considered outdated and irrelevant. Others of us, however, maintain that some things are always right or wrong and that God's Word has identified these moral absolutes.

Verse 5 points out that truly wise people know and seek to do what is right, but evil people lack a basic understanding of justice and morality. This is a basic assumption of the Wisdom Writings. Wisdom reveals how people ought to live. It reveals not only how to live but shows why doing right is the wise and prudent way to live.

Some people think that God's laws are arbitrary. That is, these people assume that God made rules in order to show us He is God. They think God is like the parent who answers a child's question about why the child is to do a certain thing, "Because I told you to!" God did tell us to do certain things and not to do certain other things, but He had good reasons for this. The bad things hurt and destroy people, families, and society. The good things promote life, health, and joy.

2. True wealth (v. 6)

6 Better is the poor that walketh in his uprightness, than he that is perverse in his ways, though he be rich.

Verses like Proverbs 3:10 seem to promise material prosperity to the righteous, but verses like Proverbs 28:6 show that this is not always true. The verse stresses that poor but righteous people have far greater wealth than wealthy sinners (see also Prov. 16:8). Whether one is rich or poor, true wealth is in an upright character. Thus, Proverbs 22:1 says, "A good name is rather to be chosen than great riches."

In fact, Proverbs 28:6 and other Bible verses warn that wealth can result in spiritual poverty. Jesus often warned of the dangers of riches (Luke 12:16–21; 16:19–31; 18:18–25). When the glorified Lord spoke to the seven churches of Asia, the Lord told the Smyrna (SMUR nuh) church that He knew about their poverty; but He added, "Thou art rich" (Rev. 2:9). The Lord said that the church at Laodicea (lay ahd ih SEE uh) thought of themselves as rich and self-sufficient; but He said, "Thou art wretched, and miserable, and poor, and blind, and naked" (Rev. 3:17).

3. Family values (v. 7)

7 Whoso keepeth the law is a wise son: but he that is a companion of riotous men shameth his father.

Here is another contrast between a wise man and a fool. The wise man obeys God's law and in the process also honors his father. By contrast, the other man makes friends with "riotous" men. His actions shame his father.

The word translated "riotous" means someone who wastes his resources and endangers his health. The word is translated "glutton" and linked with the "drunkard" in Proverbs 23:21. This man and his cronies engage in the kinds of sins against which Paul warned in Romans 13:13. Notice how many evils flow from this kind of living. The person ruins his own character. He disgraces his family name and brings grief and shame to his parents. He joins in corrupting his companions. In the process, he wastes his possessions and risks his health.

III. Sin and Retribution (Prov. 28:8–12)

1. Losing unjust gains (v. 8)

8 He that by usury and unjust gain increaseth his substance, he shall gather it for him that will pity the poor.

The Israelites were commanded not to charge interest on a loan to a fellow Israelite, although they could charge interest to foreigners (Deut. 23:19–20). The purpose of the law was to encourage help for the poor. If an Israelite could not give to the poor, at least he could make an interest-free loan (Exod. 22:25; Lev. 25:35–37). Nehemiah 5:7–11 shows that this law was often violated. Proverbs 28:8 shows that some grew wealthy by thus exploiting the poor.

Verse 8 warns that the greedy man is only gathering wealth for someone who will give generously to the poor. Verse 8 does not tell how it will happen, but it says that the greedy man's resources will be used by the good man to help the needy. Perhaps the implication is that the one who inherits his estate will be generous. The principle is set forth in the parable of the talents (Matt. 25:28–29). Unfaithful stewards lose what they had, and it is entrusted to faithful stewards.

2. Unanswered prayers (28:9)

9 He that turneth away his ear from hearing the law, even his prayer shall be abomination.

People who refuse to listen to God's law are people who live in sin. God does not hear the prayers of persistent sinners. "If I regard iniquity in my heart, the Lord will not hear me" (Ps. 66:18). Proverbs 28:9 goes a step farther; it says that such so-called prayers are "abomination." This strong word was used for what God called pagan worship.

This is a familiar theme in the Prophets. The Lord despises hypocritical worship (Amos 5:21–24). "When ye make many prayers, I will not hear: your hands are full of blood" (Isa. 1:15). By contrast, God delights in the prayers of the righteous (Prov. 15:8, 29).

3. Caught in your own trap (v. 10)

10 Whoso causeth the righteous to go astray in an evil way, he shall fall himself into his own pit: but the upright shall have good things in possession.

Some evil people delight in trying to seduce good people to join them in sin. Jesus warned of the seriousness of this sin (Matt. 18:6). Verse 10 compares such people to hunters who dig a pit to trap their game, but they end up falling into the pit. Proverbs 1:10–19 tells how criminals try to lure young men to join them, but the young men are warned that these violent men lie in "wait for their own blood" (Prov. 1:18). Proverbs 5:1–6 warns against immoral women who try to seduce the innocent. Verse 5 says of the immoral seducer, "Her feet go down to death; her steps take hold on hell."

God's wrath is sometimes expressed in personal terms in the Bible; at other times, God's wrath works through the law of sin and retribution that God has built into His universe. God allows people to reap what they sow (Gal. 6:7; see also Num. 32:23). The Book of Proverbs considers sin not only as evil but also as irrational. Sin hurts those against whom it is directed, but it also comes back to destroy the sinner himself. The last part of verse 13 presents the positive side of the moral law of God: those who sow seeds of righteousness will reap a good harvest (receive a good inheritance).

4. Folly of sin (vv. 11–12)

A rich man has an inflated view of his own wisdom, but a wise poor man sees through him (v. 11). A good ruler causes rejoicing, but an evil ruler causes people to hide (v. 12).

IV. Confession and Mercy (Prov. 28:13)

13 He that covereth his sins shall not prosper: but whoso confesseth and forsaketh them shall have mercy.

"Covereth" is used here to mean "hides." Of course, sin cannot be hidden from God nor from the sinner himself. Psalm 32:3–4 describes David's misery during the time when he tried to hide his sin. The rest of the psalm describes his joy when he finally confessed his sin and received God's forgiveness.

Verse 13 promises that God will show mercy on those who confess and forsake their sins. The word translated "covereth" in verse 13 is used in Psalm 85:2 to describe how God covers or forgives confessed sins. This is a familiar promise of the prophets (Isa. 55:6–7). The closest biblical parallel to Proverbs 28:13 is 1 John 1:8–9: "If we say that we have no sin, we deceive ourselves, and the truth is not in us. If we confess our sins, he is faithful and just to forgive us our sins, and to cleanse us from all unrighteousness."

APPLYING THE BIBLE

1. Obeying God's law. I love the story about the poor boy who was told by a man, "Son, if you tell me the truth, I'll give you a quarter." The boy answered, "I'll tell you the truth whether you give me a quarter or not." The boy was young in his walk as a Christian, but his maturity in true wisdom was apparent in that walk! In fact, his answer represents "Spiritual Graduate School!"

2. One size fits all! I heard, recently, a nationally televised debate between leading journalists about whether or not the Ten Commandments were outdated. A Christian on the panel produced a stunned silence by asking, "Which one of the Ten Commandments would, if obeyed, be detrimental to the welfare of an individual or a nation?" Apply that question to your personal life, to your family, to your church, and to your town. The question is appropriate, no matter what denominational or political or racial labels we wear. Indeed and in truth, one size fits all!

3. No such thing as truth. Hitler once said about the Ten Commandments, "The Ten Commandments have lost their validity. There is no such thing as truth, either in the moral or in the scientific scene." It was but another of the many truly insane things the German madman said, and his life demonstrated that fact.

4. Nobody knows? A group of boys in our community broke into a school and stole thousands of dollars worth of school property. Several of them had second thoughts about the escapade and asked if I would meet with the entire group and give them counsel about what to do. During the discussion, one of the boys said, angrily, "Nobody knows. Why should we confess it and get into trouble?" I informed the boys that they had already been caught! They had been caught by police officials. (One of the boys had left some blood on a window sill at the crime scene.) They had been caught by themselves—after all, *they* knew about it! They had been caught by each other. I knew about it (and thus, I had "caught" them). And they had been caught by God! Quite an audience!

5. Disregarding God. Our disregard for God—in fact, a sort of hatred for God—is evidenced by the fact that we hide our sins from others. (At least we are petrified lest others know!) Yes, we show no concern at all that God knows all about our sins!

6. The categorical imperative. The German Philosopher Immanuel Kant espoused a concept of ethical behavior called the "principle of universality"; that is, we should do that which, if done by all people, would produce a virtuous society. His statement of the principle is this: "There is therefore but one categorical imperative, namely this: Act only on that maxim whereby you can at the same time will that it should become universal law." To put it in common vernacular: What if everybody in your church treated others as you do? Or gave as you do? Or witnessed as you do? Or forgave as you do?

7. Breaking God's laws? We often speak of "breaking God's laws," but in fact, not one of God's laws has ever been broken. They have been violated, disobeyed, disregarded, and unknown, but not one has ever been broken. For instance, if a man falls off a ten-story building, he does not break the law of gravity; he proves the law of gravity! He breaks himself, not the law of gravity. Nobody ever "breaks" God's law in the sense of destroying the law. Someone put it, tongue-in-cheek, this way: "In man's struggle with the universe, the universe almost always wins." Nobody violates God's law and wins.

TEACHING THE BIBLE

- *Main Idea:* Obeying God's law is a mark of a wise person.
- *Suggested Teaching Aim:* To lead adults to become wise people by confessing their sin

A TEACHING OUTLINE

1. Use a life situation to introduce the Bible study.

2. Use a chart and group discussion to guide the search for biblical truth.

3. Use personal examination to give the truth a personal focus.

Introduce the Bible Study

Read: "Susan moved into a community that was dominated by a particular religion. She opened a store, and all of the local townspeople started trading with her. They all ran up large charge accounts. One day some representatives of the religion came to talk to her. They asked her to join their church. When Susan explained that she was already an active member in her church and did not want to change, she was told that she had two choices: either convert to their religion or face bankruptcy because they would instruct their members who owed her money not to pay their bills. Susan said . . ."[1]

Ask: How willing are we to obey God's laws when it costs us dearly? Suggest that today's lessons will explain why wise people obey God's law and foolish people don't.

Search for Biblical Truth

Ask: How do you react to the statement: "Because I said so!"? Do you feel God responds to us in this way? Why?

Say: God has established laws that protect us, not laws that deny us pleasure. A wise person is able to see that this is true.

On a chalkboard or a large sheet of paper, write the following chart, except for the italicized phrases and words:

Obey God's Laws

Scripture	Act	Result
28:4	*law forsakers*	*praise the wicked*
28:4	*law keepers*	*resist wicked*
28:5	*evil people*	*misunderstand justice*
28:5	*righteous people*	*understand justice*
28:6	*poor*	*uprightness*
28:6	*perverse*	*rich*
28:7	*law keeper*	*wise*
28:7	*gluttons/drunkard*	*shame*
28:8	*unjust gain*	*loses gain*
28:9	*lawbreakers*	*prayers not heard*
28:10	*deceiving good people*	*fall in pit*
28:10	*righteous*	*possess good things*

Ask members to open their Bibles to 28:4–5. Ask members to identify the act/persons mentioned in these verses and the results of their actions; write these on the chart.

DISCUSS: How do we know the difference between God's absolute rules and specific cultural rules?

Ask members to read 28:6 and to identify the act/persons mentioned in these verses and the results of their actions; write these on the chart.

DISCUSS: In looking back over your life the past three months, did you choose a good name rather than great riches? How do you feel about your choice(s)?

Ask members to read 28:7 and to identify the act/persons mentioned in these verses and the results of their actions; write these on the chart.

DISCUSS: In what ways does a person who is a glutton/drunkard affect others as well as himself?

Ask members to read 28:8 and to identify the act/persons mentioned in these verses and the results of their actions; write these on the chart.

DISCUSS: How do you feel about greedy people who always seem to prosper? Are you tempted to follow their path?

Ask members to read 28:9 and to identify the act/persons mentioned in these verses and the results of their actions; write these on the chart.

DISCUSS: What have you done that has made your prayers/worship an abomination to the Lord?

Ask members to read 28:10 and to identify the act/persons mentioned in these verses and the results of their actions; write these on the chart.

DISCUSS: Based upon your life in the past, do your actions show that you believe that those who sow seeds of righteousness will reap a good harvest?

Give the Truth a Personal Focus

Ask members to read 28:13. Say: If you have failed to obey God's laws and tried to cover your sins, will you confess them now and receive God's mercy?

---

1. James E. Taulman, *Help! I Need an Idea* (Nashville: Broadman Press, 1987), 119.

AUGUST

2

1998

Wisdom or Foolishness

Basic Passage: Proverbs 8

Focal Passages: Proverbs 8:1–11, 33–36

At several points in the early chapters of Proverbs, wisdom is personified as a woman. Proverbs 1:20–33, for example, describes wisdom as a "she," not an "it." Wisdom cried in the streets like a prophet warning young men against the dangers of turning from the fear of the Lord. Proverbs 8 is a longer description of wisdom in personal terms. Again wisdom cries in the street, but this time she shares the good news of what she offers to those who heed her call.

➧ **Study Aim:** *To describe wisdom's message and how she presented it*

STUDYING THE BIBLE

OUTLINE AND SUMMARY

I. Wisdom's Call (Prov. 8:1–11)
  1. Seeks all people where they are (vv. 1–5)
  2. Speaks what is right and true (vv. 6–11)

II. Wisdom's Rewards (Prov. 8:12–21)
  1. Strength for goodness and godliness (vv. 12–16)
  2. Guidance in righteousness and justice (vv. 17–21)

III. Wisdom's Role in Creation (Prov. 8:22–31)
  1. Prior to creation (vv. 22–26)
  2. With God in creation (vv. 27–31)

IV. Wisdom's Invitation (Prov. 8:32–36)
  1. Call to listen and watch (vv. 32–34)
  2. Life or death issue (vv. 35–36)

Wisdom goes to places where people congregate and calls all, but especially the simple and fools (vv. 1–5). She speaks a message that is right, true, and plain (vv. 6–11). Wisdom hates evil and provides strength for wise rulers (vv. 12–16). She richly rewards with righteousness and justice (vv. 17–21). Wisdom existed prior to creation (vv. 22–26). She rejoiced with God over His good creation (vv. 27–31). Wisdom earnestly calls for people to hear and heed (vv. 32–34). She promises life to those who find her, but warns of self-inflicted wrong and death for those who refuse her (vv. 35–36).

I. Wisdom's Call (Prov. 8:1–11)

1. Seeks all people where they are (vv. 1–5)

1 Doth not wisdom cry? and understanding put forth her voice?

2 She standeth in the top of high places, by the way in the places of the paths.

3 She crieth at the gates, at the entry of the city, at the coming in at the doors.

4 Unto you, O men, I call: and my voice is to the sons of men.
5 O ye simple, understand wisdom: and, ye fools, be ye of an understanding heart.

Notice the "her" and "she" in these verses. "I" will appear in verse 6 as wisdom actually begins to speak. Verses 1–5 are the wise teacher or father's description of wisdom as a woman.

The immediate background is a description of an evil woman in Proverbs 7. An overview of chapter 7 helps us understand chapter 8. The father tells his son to claim wisdom as his sister in order that she might keep him from becoming prcy to the evil woman (7:1–5). An immoral woman watches for an innocent young man and seduces him under cover of darkness (7:6–13). She offers him the pleasures of forbidden love (7:14–20). After yielding to her wiles, he is led like a dumb animal to the slaughter (7:21–23). The wise father warns young men not to follow the immoral woman to doom (7:24–27).

The picture of wisdom as a woman is in striking contrast to the woman of chapter 7. Rather than sneaking about in the dark, wisdom cries aloud in the daylight for all to hear. Verses 1–3 picture wisdom taking her stand at places where people congregate and can hear her message. Bible scholars disagree about the exact meaning of "high places" in verse 2a. Various suggestions include city walls, hill tops, and highways. All agree that the "high places" were some place where many would hear her message. The last part of verse 2 may refer to busy intersections or to thoroughfares.

Verse 3 refers to the city gates. The gates of a city are mentioned often in the Old Testament. This location played a key role in many aspects of community life. The elders held court at the city gates (Deut. 22:15). Legal contracts were witnessed there (Ruth 4:1–10). Grievances were spoken there to public officials (2 Sam. 15:2). Prophets preached at the gates (1 Kings 22:10). The gates provided a place for sharing news and gossip (Ps. 69:12).

Wisdom went where people were and delivered her message to everyone. The words "men" and "sons of men" in verse 4 show that she spoke not just to the intellectuals and well-educated but also to the common people. Wisdom's message was especially addressed to those most in need of wisdom. Verse 5 mentions two groups: the "simple" and "fools." The "simple" were the inexperienced who were open to whatever influence reached them first. The "fools" were dull people who were insensitive to moral truth.

2. Speaks what is right and true (vv. 6–11)

6 Hear; for I will speak of excellent things; and the opening of my lips shall be right things.
7 For my mouth shall speak truth; and wickedness is an abomination to my lips.
8 All the words of my mouth are in righteousness; there is nothing froward or perverse in them.
9 They are all plain to him that understandeth, and right to them that find knowledge.

10 Receive my instruction, and not silver; and knowledge rather than choice gold.

11 For wisdom is better than rubies; and all the things that may be desired are not to be compared to it.

Notice "I" in verse 6 and scattered throughout the rest of the chapter. Wisdom herself speaks. Wisdom begins, as did the wise father, by calling for listeners to truly "hear" (1:8; 4:1). Wisdom's message begins and ends with calls to "hear" (vv. 32–33).

Three words are key in verses 6–9: "right" ("righteousness"), "truth," and "plain." Wisdom speaks about what is right, true, and understandable. Her message is not primarily intellectual but moral. She is concerned about people knowing and doing what is right. Of course, wisdom teaches that doing what is right is the wise and rational way to live; so any truly thinking person will choose this way rather than the irrational, destructive way of doing wrong.

The Book of Proverbs contains guidance about many specific areas of daily life. Earlier we looked at being a good neighbor. During the next four sessions, we will consider work, speech, anger, and family. In each area, wisdom is concerned with doing what is right.

Wisdom's words are true. Unlike the immoral woman of chapter 7, she does not use lies or half-truths to win people to her way. Wickedness is an abomination to her lips. She speaks truth with nothing crooked or perverse.

The word "plain" in verse 9 may mean either easy for the wise to understand or becoming understandable to those who commit themselves to her way. Both principles are taught elsewhere in the Bible: (1) Those who know God's divine wisdom are able to understand His message as plain and straightforward. Paul, for example, said that the cross seems foolish when judged by worldly wisdom, but believers know that it represents the power and wisdom of God (1 Cor. 1:18–31). (2) Outsiders can discover the truth of God's wisdom by committing themselves to live by it. Jesus said, "If any man will do his will, he shall know of the doctrine, whether it be of God, or whether I speak of myself" (John 7:17).

Proverbs 8:10–11 uses similar words as Proverbs 3:14–15. Each passage praises wisdom as being more valuable than silver, gold, precious stones, or anything that people might desire.

II. Wisdom's Rewards (Prov. 8:12–21)

1. Strength for goodness and godliness (vv. 12–16)

True wisdom is as shrewd as any worldly wisdom (v. 12); but because it is based on the fear of the Lord, true wisdom hates all evil (v. 13). Wisdom shows her insight and strength (v. 14) by enabling rulers to rule with righteousness and justice (vv. 15–16).

2. Guidance in righteousness and justice (vv. 17–21)

Those who love wisdom easily find her (v. 17). They receive her rich rewards. These riches (v. 18) and treasures (v. 21) are primarily guidance in the paths of righteousness and justice (v. 20). These are declared more precious than the most precious of earthly treasures (v. 19).

III. Wisdom's Role in Creation (Prov. 8:22–31)

1. Prior to creation (vv. 22–26)

The identity of wisdom in verses 22–31 has been a matter of scholarly debate. Some say that wisdom is pictured here as a heavenly being, perhaps even the second Person of the Trinity. Others believe wisdom is an attribute of God that has been personified to make a point. God possessed wisdom in the beginning before the earth was made (vv. 22–23); so she existed prior to the fountains, mountains, and fields of the earth (vv. 24–26).

2. With God in creation (vv. 27–31)

Wisdom was with God when He created the universe and the earth (vv. 27–29). Wisdom not only witnessed God's creation but also rejoiced with Him over His good creation of all things, including human beings (vv. 30–31).

IV. Wisdom's Invitation (Prov. 8:32–36)

1. Call to listen and watch (vv. 32–34)

33 Hear instruction, and be wise, and refuse it not.

34 Blessed is the man that heareth me, watching daily at my gates, waiting at the posts of my doors.

Just as wisdom's message began with a call to "hear" (v. 6), so her final invitation has a double emphasis on "hearken" (v. 32) and "hear" (v. 33). The divine call to hear always includes an assumption that the one who hears will obey. A blessing is pronounced on those who keep wisdom's ways (v. 32). The "simple" and the "fools" were especially in mind (v. 5). They were called to hear and be wise. They were warned not to refuse to hear.

Verse 34 begins with another blessing pronounced on those who hear wisdom. The setting for wisdom's message has been the busy places where people congregate. Wisdom took her message to them where they were. Verse 34 changes the analogy to that of the home of a wise teacher. People need to be so eager to hear wisdom speak that they will wait and watch expectantly at her door so they can speak with her when she comes out—like students lining up after a class session to talk further with a popular professor.

This may sound like a contradiction, yet the Bible teaches not only that God seeks us (Luke 15:3–7; 19:10) but also that we must seek Him (Isa. 55:6–7). The stress on seeking God or wisdom does not imply that God or wisdom is hard to find, only that each person must decide to respond to the divine call.

2. Life or death issue (vv. 35–36)

35 For whoso findeth me findeth life, and shall obtain favour of the LORD.

36 But he that sinneth against me wrongeth his own soul: all they that hate me love death.

No one can remain neutral. Each must choose, and the choice determines life or death. The person who finds wisdom finds life in the process, and life is determined by a right relationship with God. By contrast, the person who sins against wisdom ends up wronging himself. To hate wisdom is to love death. Proverbs 8:35–36 thus joins a host of other life-or-death Bible passages (Deut. 30:19; Ezek. 33:11; Rom. 6:23).

Wisdom is used here as meaning God and the way of life He intends for human beings. Those who live in harmony with God and His way find life. Those who continue to go their own way without God and to spurn His way meet death. This is the ultimate example of the law of sin and retribution. The death that comes from sin is not an arbitrary punishment inflicted by a vengeful God. It is the inevitable consequence of choosing a way that leads to death.

APPLYING THE BIBLE

1. Wisdom and humility. If we are to pursue wisdom successfully, we must admit that we don't yet possess it all. In *The Pilgrim's Regress,* C. S. Lewis wrote, "'And what is this valley called?' 'We call it now simply Wisdom's Valley: but the oldest maps mark it as the Valley of Humiliation.'" Wisdom and humiliation are located in the same area!

2. A feminine touch. The Book of Proverbs personifies wisdom as a woman. In the New Testament, the Greek word for wisdom (*sophia*) is in the feminine gender.

3. A poet's prayer.

From the laziness that is content with half-truth,
From the fear that shrinks from new truth,
From the arrogance that thinks it knows all truth,
O God of Truth, deliver us.

4. Not so fast! A young man who had just received his college degree rushed out and exclaimed, "Here I am, World: I have my A.B.!" The World replied, "Sit down, Son, and I'll teach you the rest of the alphabet."

5. God's infinite wisdom. One of the great benefits of listening to God is that it gives us an objective view of reality. We leave the thimble of our own limited amount of truth and find ourselves upon God's great ocean of unlimited truth. (Or, to use Malcolm Muggeridge's phrase, we leave the tiny dark prison cells of our own egos for God's infinite universe.)

6. Self-centered or God-centered? Contrast biblical wisdom with these words of Shirley MacLaine in an interview with the *Washington Post:*

> The most pleasurable journey you can take is through yourself . . . the only sustaining love is with yourself. . . . When you look back on your life and try to figure out where you've been and where you're going, when you look at your work, your love affairs, your marriages, your children, your pain, your happiness—when you examine all that closely, what you really find out is that the only person you really go to bed with is yourself. . . . The only thing you have is working to the consummation of your own identity. And that's what I've been trying to do all my life.

7. Alone forever. Imagine being alone with yourself, totally, for eternity! The following lines are from John Milton's *Paradise Lost:*

Which way shall I fly.
Infinite wrath and infinite despair?
Which way I fly is hell; myself am hell.

8. Obeying the truth. Gilbert Chesterton has a marvelous line: "The reason for opening the mind is precisely the same for opening the mouth—to close it on something solid once in a while!" The Bible always calls us to a practical and personal application of truth. In fact, we are told throughout the Bible that it is better to be exposed to truth and not obey it than it is not to know truth at all!

9. Memorable lines.

- No matter how wealthy one is, wisdom must always be purchased on the installment plan.
- "Not ignorance, but the ignorance of ignorance is the death of knowledge" (Alfred North Whitehead).
- "The sun cannot show herself to a blind man" (Charles H. Spurgeon).

TEACHING THE BIBLE

- *Main Idea:* Finding wisdom is a matter of life and death.
- *Suggested Teaching Aim:* To lead adults to choose to follow God's wisdom so they may gain life

A TEACHING OUTLINE

1. Use a quarter poster and a collage to introduce the Bible study.
2. Use a strip poster to guide the search for biblical truth.
3. Use Bible search and group discussion to search for biblical truth.
4. Use personal examination to give the truth a personal focus.

Introduce the Bible Study

Use the quarter poster to introduce the new unit. Point out that this unit continues the study in Proverbs. This unit is entitled: "Two Ways—the Way of Wisdom and the Way of Foolishness."

IN ADVANCE, look through the newspaper and find articles that describe foolish behavior. Make a collage of these articles. Read the headlines and suggest that God gives us wisdom to avoid the foolish way as we live in the world.

Search for Biblical Truth

IN ADVANCE, make two strip posters by using roman numerals I and IV from the outline in "Outline and Summary." Place the first poster on the wall.

Point out that wisdom is described as a woman, possibly to contrast it with the foolishness of the evil woman in chapter 7 who seeks to seduce young men. Ask members to open their Bibles to 8:1–5 and answer these questions: From where does wisdom call? (High places and gates—where people congregate.) To whom does wisdom call? (To all people—particularly those who are inexperienced or insensitive to moral truth.) Use "Studying the Bible" to explain these answers.

Ask members to skim 8:6–11 and answer this question: What is the first command given by wisdom in these verses? (Hear.) Point out that *hear* in the Bible always has the sense of hear and obey.

Suggest that 8:6–9 uses six words to describe the manner in which wisdom speaks. Ask members to identify these six words. (v. 6, excellent, right; v. 7, truth; v. 8, righteousness; v. 9, plain, right.) Use "Studying the Bible" to explain "right," "truth," and "plain." Ask: With what did wisdom compare her teachings?

DISCUSS: Do you really believe that wisdom is better than silver, gold, and rubies? What in your actions this past week would show that you believe this? that you don't believe this?

Place the second poster strip on the wall. Ask members to read silently wisdom's invitation in 8:33–36. Ask, If you changed the person speaking from wisdom to God, what difference would it make in these verses? How hard is it to find God or wisdom? What are the choices people face in choosing wisdom? (Life or death.)

Ask three members to look up and read aloud Deuteronomy 30:19; Ezekiel 33:11; and Romans 6:23.

Give the Truth a Personal Focus

Ask: Based on this lesson, are you a wise person? Have you found God and His wisdom as the guiding principle of your life? Will you respond to Him today and let His wisdom guide you so you will not make any foolish decisions about eternal life?

Hard Work and Laziness

AUGUST

9

1998

Basic Passages: Proverbs 6:6–8; 10:4–5; 13:4; 15:19; 18:9; 20:4; 24:30–34

Focal Passages: Proverbs 6:6–8; 10:4–5; 13:4; 15:19; 18:9; 20:4; 24:30–34

The ancient Greeks despised work. The ideal for them was a life of leisure. By contrast, the Hebrews saw work as a blessing and duty. This fact is nowhere so clear as in the repeated hammer blows commending work and condemning laziness that are scattered throughout the Book of Proverbs. Some of these verses have been selected for this lesson. The references are in no particular sequence in Proverbs, and much repetition is used of the main themes: praise of work and the folly of laziness.

Study Aim: *To explain why work is a blessing and laziness is a sin*

STUDYING THE BIBLE

OUTLINE AND SUMMARY

I. Blessing of Work (Prov. 6:6–8; 10:4–5; 13:4)

1. Lessons from the ant (6:6–8)

2. A wise son (10:5)

3. Fruits of work (10:4; 13:4)

II. Sin of Laziness (Prov. 15:19; 18:9; 20:4; 24:30–34)

1. A moral issue (15:19)

2. Good intentions not enough (24:30–33)

3. Self-inflicted destruction (18:9; 20:4; 24:34)

The ant teaches lessons of hard work and foresight (6:6–8). A wise son works when it is time to work and does his part in helping his family (10:5). Diligent work provides support for those who work and their families (10:4; 13:4). Laziness is contrasted with righteousness (15:19). A weed-infested field often testifies to a person who keeps postponing doing the needed work (24:30–33). Poverty is often self-inflicted destruction (18:9; 20:4; 24:34).

I. Blessing of Work (Prov. 6:6–8; 10:4–5; 13:4)

1. Lessons from the ant (6:6–8)

6 Go to the ant, thou sluggard; consider her ways, and be wise:

7 Which having no guide, overseer, or ruler,

8 Provideth her meat in the summer, and gathereth her food in the harvest.

The noun "sluggard" appears in the Old Testament only in Proverbs. The noun comes from a verb meaning to be sluggish or to delay. Thus, the word refers to a lazy person who tends to delay doing any work. The sluggard is told to be wise by learning lessons for life from the ant. Job 12:7 says, "Ask now the beasts, and they shall teach thee; and the fowls of the air, and they shall tell thee." Proverbs 30:18–19, 24–31 contains lessons from the ant and a number of other living creatures. Proverbs 6:7–8 notes two lessons about work to learn from the ant.

First of all, the ant is by nature a worker. The casual observer sees no system of organization within the ant colony; the ant appears to work on her own with no direction to do so. Even if the ant colony is more organized than appears, ants are still by nature workers. According to God's plan for humanity, people also were created to have work as a part of life. The Bible views work as a blessing that was part of God's good creation (Gen. 1:28: 2:15). Only after sin came did work become toil (Gen. 3:17–19). Even so, God calls people back to His original pattern for human life. Jesus said that both He and His Father are workers (John 5:17). Jesus was a carpenter (Mark 6:3); Paul was a tent maker (Acts 18:3).

Second, the ant has the foresight to lay aside during the harvest for the season when food will be needed. This kind of foresight is commended. Jesus seemed to warn against it in Matthew 6:25, 27–28, 31, 34, especially when He said to "take no thought" for tomorrow. However, a better translation is to "be not anxious" about tomorrow. Jesus was not warning against careful planning but against the kind of worldly anxiety that contradicts trust in God. Likewise, James 4:13–16 does not forbid planning for the future; it forbids presuming that one can live and plan without God.

2. A wise son (10:5)

> **5 He that gathereth in summer is a wise son: but he that sleepeth in harvest is a son that causeth shame.**

Many verses on work contrast a wise worker with a foolish sluggard. One son works during the summer harvest to lay up stores for the winter; the other son sleeps during the harvesttime. The first son is a model of good work in two ways.

First, the wise son lived according to the cycles and seasons of life. Ecclesiastes 3:1–11 says that there is a time for everything. God gives us time to sleep; however, days of a ripe harvest are not a time to sleep but to work. The Fourth Commandment commands both work and rest. It was designed to free people from the tyranny of working seven days a week, but it also commanded working six days (Exod. 20:8–11; Deut. 5:12–15). Living according to God's plan calls for a balance of work, rest, and worship. Workaholics go to one extreme; sluggards go to the other.

Second, a son in that day was an indispensable part of the family work force. In a rural society, every family member was needed during planting and harvesting. Otherwise, the entire family suffered. Thus, the son who slept during harvest failed and shamed himself and his family.

3. Fruits of work (10:4; 13:4)

> **10:4 He becometh poor that dealeth with a slack hand: but the hand of the diligent maketh rich.**
>
> **13:4 The soul of the sluggard desireth, and hath nothing: but the soul of the diligent shall be made fat.**

Proverbs 10:4 says that the person with a slack hand becomes poor, and the one with diligent hands becomes rich. Proverbs 13:4 says that although the sluggard wants to have the things he needs, he has nothing, but the diligent person has plenty of food. In other words, hard work leads to wealth and food, but laziness leads to poverty and hunger. Stated more generally, the verses teach that a worker takes care of his own needs and the needs of his family.

The teaching of these verses needs to be seen in light of other passages about poverty and hunger. All poverty and hunger is not caused by the person being too lazy to work. Other verses in Proverbs make clear that wealth sometimes is the result of ill-gotten gains (28:8) and that generous people need to help the poor (21:13; 22:9). The Old Testament commands care for the poor and the helpless groups in society, especially widows and orphans (Deut. 24:10–22).

The early churches were diligent in taking care of the needs of poor members. The classic view of Christian work is expressed in Ephesians 4:28, "Let him that stole steal no more: but rather let him labour, working with his hands the thing that is good, that he may have to give to him that needeth." Notice that Paul said the purpose of work was to create something good and to have something to give to the needy. Elsewhere, Paul also stressed taking care of the needs of one's own family (1 Tim. 5:8). Paul, of course, took a dim view of able-bodied people who quit work and then expected the church to support them. In 2 Thessalonians 3:7–12, Paul said that "if any would not work, neither should he eat" (v. 10).

II. Sin of Laziness (Prov. 15:19; 18:9; 20:4; 24:30–34)

1. A moral issue (15:19)

19 The way of the slothful man is as an hedge of thorns: but the way of the righteous is made plain.

Here is another contrast. One person's actions build a hedge of thorns across the road of his life. The other person's actions result in a way that is free of self-imposed obstacles. "Made plain" literally means "is cast up." The picture is of building a road by casting up dirt to make a smooth surface (see Isa. 40:3–4).

The two people are characterized as "slothful" and "righteous." Ordinarily, the sluggard or slothful person is contrasted with the diligent or hard-working person. However, in this case, the lazy person is contrasted with the upright person. In other words, whether one works or not is a moral issue of right and wrong. The passage does not use the word *sin* to describe laziness, but that is the implication of contrasting laziness with uprightness.

2. Good intentions not enough (24:30–33)

30 I went by the field of the slothful, and by the vineyard of the man void of understanding;

31 And, lo, it was all grown over with thorns, and nettles had covered the face thereof, and the stone wall thereof was broken down.

32 Then I saw, and considered it well: I looked upon it, and received instruction.

33 Yet a little sleep, a little slumber, a little folding of the hands to sleep:

The writer describes observing a field and vineyard. They showed no signs of being cared for. Thorns flourished and covered the land and everything on it. The stone walls had fallen down. Verse 30 describes this as the property of a slothful or lazy man and a "man void of understanding." He was not only lazy but foolish.

Some translations place quotation marks around the words of verse 33. The assumption is that the writer only quoted what the slothful man said to explain his neglect. Other translations assume that the writer is being ironic and saying, "Go ahead and take your nap; go ahead and sleep" (GNB). In either case, verse 33 expresses how the lazy person looked at life. He seemed to have good intentions of getting up and doing the work, but first he wanted a little more rest. He always found excuses to postpone doing the work; and as a result, the work was never done.

3. Self-inflicted destruction (18:9; 20:4; 24:34)

24:34 So shall thy poverty come as one that travelleth; and thy want as an armed man.

Proverbs 24:33–34 is similar to Proverbs 6:10–11. Some scholars translate "an armed man" as "a beggar." The Hebrew word apparently has either meaning. If it means a robber, the idea is of the swift ruin that comes to the well-intentioned man who never gets around to working his land. If it means a beggar, the stress is on a slower but equally destructive result. The picture is of poverty clinging to one's life like a beggar who hangs around the house and always wants more. In either case, the result is destructive.

Poverty is personified either as an armed robber or as a beggar, but who is to blame for poverty? Proverbs 20:4 shows that this kind of poverty is a self-inflicted plight.

20:4 The sluggard will not plow by reason of the cold; therefore shall he beg in harvest, and have nothing.

The land of the Bible has two seasons, a hot and dry summer from May to September and a cool, moderately rainy season from October to April. Genesis 8:22 calls these "seedtime and harvest, and cold and heat." Plowing began when the early rains softened the hard, dry earth. This was usually in October or November. Since cooler weather came with the rains, the plowman sometimes had to endure a cold wind. The sluggard in Proverbs 20:4 failed to plow during the season for plowing, using the cold weather as an excuse.

When harvest season arrived in the summer, the man had no crops to harvest. The word translated "beg" means "seeks." This may mean that he begged of his neighbors. More likely, however, the picture is the man seeking crops in his own fields and finding none. In either case, who was to blame? He was the one who had failed to plow and plant during the right season. Therefore, he could not expect to find crops where he had sowed no seed.

18:9 He also that is slothful in his work is brother to him that is a great waster.

"Great waster" means literally "possessor of destruction." This is a serious charge. The lazy person is brother to the destroyer. Lazy people are not being accused of being murderers or robbers, but they are accused of being kin to them because their laziness deprives the person, his family, and others of what they need. To put it another way, laziness is a sin against the God who gave work as a blessing, against those who need the fruits of one's work, and against oneself who falls so far short of God-given potential.

APPLYING THE BIBLE

1. The godliness of work. In the beginning of history, God gave Adam and Eve work to do ("The LORD God put him into the garden of Eden to dress it and to keep it" [Gen. 2:15]). In the end of history, in heaven, God will assign work for us to do ("His servants shall serve him" [Rev. 22:3]). Throughout the interim period, God commands us to work ("Let him that stole steal no more: but rather let him labour, working with his hands the thing which is good, that he may have to give to him that needeth" [Eph. 4:28]).

2. Fear of work. I have a friend who says that the bad thing about being lazy is that you can never enjoy taking a day off! (By the way: a new word is making the rounds these days; it is *ergophobia,* that is, the fear of work! Woe to those who are so afflicted.)

3. Goofing off. Only one in four American workers say they are giving their best effort at work. Most admit to spending about 20 percent of their time at work goofing off. Almost half say they have called in sick when they were not sick.[1] How does that differ from stealing money from one's employer?

4. Work and love. "Work is love made visible. And if you cannot work with love but only with distaste, it is better that you should leave your work and sit at the gate of the temple and take alms of those who work with joy" (Kahlil Gibran).

5. Work prevents rigor mortis from setting in! "The fatigue of older persons is seen most commonly among persons who do not have enough to do. Too often they feel that their life's work is done. Their fatigue has its origin in boredom and loss of interest and incentive. Over and over, when a crisis arises, or something of deep interest comes along, these individuals lose their fatigue" (Andrew Blackwood).

6. The blessing of work. "Thank God every morning when you get up that you have something to do that day which must be done, whether you like it or not. Being forced to work, and forced to do your best, will breed in you temperance and self-control, diligence and strength of will, cheerfulness and content, and a hundred virtues which the idle never know" (Charles Kingsley).

7. The therapy of work. Psychotherapist Dr. William T. Glasser, in his book *Reality Therapy,* writes, "The more responsible a person is, the healthier he is—the less responsible, the less healthy." Glasser's essential position about mental health is: There is no mental illness, only varying degrees of irresponsibility. Glasser might not be privy to all the truth about that subject, but no Bible student can deny that, from one cover to the other, God affirms the therapy of work; it is as if we are made to work.

8. Helping the unemployed. One of the most exciting ministries of our church in recent years has been to help the unemployed in our membership find gainful employment. What sort of help could your church—or class—give in that regard?

TEACHING THE BIBLE

- *Main Idea:* God made work a blessing and laziness a sin.
- *Suggested Teaching Aim:* To lead adults to explain why work is a blessing and laziness is a sin

A TEACHING OUTLINE

1. *Use an illustration to introduce the Bible Study.*
2. *Use a chart to guide the search for biblical truth.*
3. *Use a group activity to get members to examine the text.*
4. *Use a prayer to give the truth a personal focus.*

Introduce the Bible Study

Use "The godliness of work" in "Applying the Bible" to introduce the Bible's concept of work.

Search for Biblical Truth

On a chalkboard or a large sheet of paper, write *Wise* and *Sluggards* at the head of two columns. Read aloud Job 12:7. Say: The Bible often uses animals as examples or lessons for humans. Ask members to turn in their Bibles to Proverbs 30:18–19, 24–31 and identify the different animals that are mentioned there from which humans can learn a lesson. Suggest that today's lesson includes only one of these: ants. Ask members to open their Bibles to Proverbs 6:6–8 and ask them to summarize in one or two words how the wise (industrious) and the sluggard (lazy) respond. Write these descriptions on the chart.

Point out that ants by nature are workers, and that God has created us to work. Ask members to list some of the occupations of people mentioned in the Bible.

Ask members to look at 10:5 and contrast the wise (works, stores food) and the sluggard (lazy, refuses to save). Read Exodus 20:8–11 aloud: Ask: What does this Commandment teach about work? rest? workaholism? laziness?

Ask members to look at 10:4 and 13:4 and contrast the wise (diligent, needs satisfied) and the sluggard (lazy, has nothing). Ask: Is hard work always a guarantee of financial success? Is all poverty and hunger caused by laziness? What is the Bible's view of helping the poor?

IN ADVANCE, make a poster by writing the words of Ephesians 4:28 on a large sheet of paper. Suggest that this verse expresses the classic view of Christian work. Ask: According to this verse, what is the purpose of work? (To have something to share with the needy.)

IN ADVANCE, make the following poster strips:

1. A moral issue (Prov. 15:19)
2. Good intentions not enough (Prov. 24:30–33)
3. Self-inflicted destruction (Prov. 18:9; 20:4; 24:34)

Cut apart the Scripture references and the titles; place them on the wall at random. Assign a third of the class to find the appropriate Scripture for each heading. Ask groups to go to the wall and remove the heading and Scripture reference when they have identified the correct Scripture.

Ask Group 1 to place its heading with Scripture reference on the wall and read the Scripture. Summarize this verse by saying that the use of the word "righteous" makes whether one works a moral issue of right and wrong.

Ask Group 2 to place its heading and Scripture reference on the wall and read the Scripture. Read the following from the Contemporary English Version: "I once walked by the field and the vineyard of a lazy fool. Thorns and weeds were everywhere, and the stone wall had fallen down. When I saw this, it taught me a lesson: Sleep a little. Doze a little. Fold your hands and twiddle your thumbs. Suddenly poverty hits you and everything is gone!"[2]

Ask Group 3 to place its heading and Scripture reference on the wall and read the Scriptures. Say: Laziness is a sin against the God who gave work as a blessing, against those who need the fruits of one's work, and against oneself who falls so far short of God-given potential.

Give the Truth a Personal Focus

Write the word *ergophobia* on a chalkboard (see "Goofing off" in "Applying the Bible"). Explain that the word means "fear of work." Explain that the Bible teaches a proper balance between work and rest. Both have God's sanction and blessing when used in the proper balance. Close with a prayer of thanksgiving for both.

---

1. Reported in *The Day America Told the Truth.*
2. *Contemporary English Version* (New York: American Bible Society, 1992).

AUGUST
16
1998

Helpful and Harmful Speech

Basic Passages: Proverbs 11:12–13; 12:18; 13:3; 15:1–2, 23, 28; 16:24; 17:27; 21:23; 26:21, 28

Focal Passages: Proverbs 11:12–13; 12:18: 13:3; 15:1–2, 23, 28; 16:24; 17:27; 21:23; 26:21, 28

What people say is another strong theme in the Book of Proverbs. Like work, words are an area of practical wisdom for everyday life. The references are scattered throughout the book. Most of these verses have three features: (1) the kind of persons who are speaking, (2) the way they use words, and (3) the consequences of what they say. Words have great power to help or to harm; therefore, wise people will be careful to speak helpful words.

➧ **Study Aim:** *To distinguish between helpful and harmful words in their own speech*

STUDYING THE BIBLE

OUTLINE AND SUMMARY

I. Watch What You Say (Prov. 11:12–13; 12:18; 13:3; 15:28; 17:27; 21:23)

1. Power of words (12:18)

2. Exercising restraint (13:3; 15:28; 17:27; 21:23)

3. When silence is golden (11:12–13)

II. Use Helpful, Not Harmful Speech (Prov. 15:1–2, 23; 16:24; 26:21, 28)

1. Harmful speech (26:21, 28)

2. Helpful speech (15:23; 16:24)

3. Striking contrasts (15:1–2)

Words can either wound or heal (12:18). Wise people, therefore, learn to use restraint in what they say (13:3; 15:28; 17:27; 21:23). Sometimes silence is the best policy (11:12–13). Contentious and lying words cause great harm (26:21, 28). Pleasant and appropriate words bring joy and healing (15:23; 16:24). Words can be harsh or soft, wise or foolish (15:1–2).

I. Watch What You Say (Prov. 11:12–13; 12:18; 13:3; 15:28; 17:27; 21:23)

1. Power of words (12:18)

18 There is that speaketh like the piercings of a sword: but the tongue of the wise is health.

The word translated "speaketh" has the idea of speaking rashly. Impulsive speaking is the opposite of careful, thoughtful speech. Such words often wound and kill as surely as does a sword. By contrast, the speech of a wise person brings health and healing.

What people say has great power to help or to hurt. As Proverbs 18:21 says, "Death and life are in the power of the tongue." Jesus said that each person will give account for "every idle word" on judgment day (Matt. 12:36). The Hebrews believed that words are extensions of the human personality. Thus once spoken, words go forth to accomplish their purpose—be it good or evil. After words have been spoken, they cannot be retrieved; they are already at work.

2. Exercising restraint (13:3; 15:28; 17:27; 21:23)

13:3 He that keepeth his mouth keepeth his life: but he that openeth wide his lips shall have destruction.

21:23 Whoso keepeth his mouth and his tongue keepeth his soul from troubles.

The word translated "keepeth" in 13:3 means to "guard." The word translated "keepeth" in 21:23 means to "watch" or to "preserve." Wise people are to guard or watch what they say. The opposite kind of person is "he that openeth wide his lips." Some people enter every situation with an open mouth. Instead of carefully watching what they say, a steady flow of words comes from their mouths. Such undisciplined speech gets them and others into trouble.

15:28 The heart of the righteous studieth to answer: but the mouth of the wicked poureth out evil things.

The word translated "studieth" means "meditate." The same word is found in Psalm 1:2, "His delight is in the law of the LORD; and in his law doth he meditate day and night." In other words, righteous people give careful thought to what they say. By contrast, the mouth of the wicked spews forth whatever evil happens to be in their minds at the time.

17:27 He that hath knowledge spareth his words: and a man of understanding is of an excellent spirit.

Verse 28 says that even a fool who remains silent may appear to be wise. If verses 27 and 28 have any connection, it may be that the person with knowledge is a person of few words and also knows when to say nothing at all. People who are sure of themselves don't need to prove anything. Thus they can weigh carefully everything they say. These four verses are some of many in Proverbs that counsel people to exercise restraint in what they say.

3. When silence is golden (11:12–13)

12 He that is void of wisdom despiseth his neighbour: but a man of understanding holdeth his peace.

13 A talebearer revealeth secrets: but he that is of a faithful spirit concealeth the matter.

Ecclesiastes 3:7 says that there is "a time to keep silence, and a time to speak." Proverbs 11:12–13 gives two examples of times when silence is the best policy. Verse 12 contrasts a man without sense who despises his neighbor with a sensible person who has learned when to keep his mouth shut. People who despise their neighbors show their hatred in a variety of ways. Since the contrast in verse 12 is with a person who keeps silent, many translators assume that the hatred in this case is expressed with words. Jesus described how people who hate others express their hatred with various kinds of verbal abuse (Matt. 5:21–22).

Belittling others is a familiar form of this sin. Since it seems more innocent than some of the others, many people use a "put-down" as a form of verbal abuse. Unfortunately, the victims of such put-downs are often family members. Parents put down their children. Spouses belittle each other with words. The opposite of belittling is encouraging and affirming others.

If a person must choose between verbal abuse and silence, the wise person will choose to remain silent. If verse 11 has any connection with verse 9, the context may be a situation in which a person has been hurt by the words of someone else. In such a situation, we are tempted to retaliate with words that hurt the person who has hurt us. Verse 12 counsels that we hold our peace.

Verse 13 contrasts a talebearer or gossip with a trustworthy person who remains silent rather than share another person's secrets. The context may be that a good person hears someone gossiping. How should good people respond when they hear gossip? They should not pass it on. If they say anything about it at all, they will go in love to the person accused of some sin and practice what Galatians 6:1 teaches. More likely, the situation in verse 13 is one in which one person has told another something in confidence. The gossip can't wait to spread the secret. The trustworthy confidant maintains the trust by remaining silent.

Christian friends surely ought to be able to trust one another with secrets. How can we bear one another's burdens if we don't know what the burdens are? However, telling others of a personal burden is risky. Some prayer groups become gossip centers hiding behind a pious front. Christians must learn to be able to hear the secret burdens of others without telling anyone but God.

II. Use Helpful, Not Harmful Speech (Prov. 15:1–2, 23; 16:24; 26:21, 28)

1. Harmful speech (26:21, 28)

21 As coals are to burning coals, and wood to fire; so is a contentious man to kindle strife.

28 A lying tongue hateth those that are afflicted by it; and a flattering mouth worketh ruin.

The word "contentious" means one who causes strife or contention. Such a person is a troublemaker who starts trouble and then keeps it going with words that incite and provoke others. Such a person is to strife what coals and wood are to fire. That is, he keeps fueling and fanning the flames of strife. In the classic biblical passage on the use of the tongue, James compared the tongue to a spark that sets an entire forest ablaze (James 3:5–6).

Verse 28 warns against the sin of lying. This deadly sin is motivated by hatred and leads to pain and affliction. Scholars debate the exact meaning of the word translated "afflicted." It may mean "crushed," or it may mean "bruised." In either case, damage is done by lying. The Ninth Commandment condemns lying about one's neighbor (Exod. 20:16;

Deut. 5:20). This includes not only bearing false witness in a court but also spreading slanderous gossip. Both are deadly sins. Perjury can result in actual death. Gossip can destroy another's reputation and life.

Ongoing human relationships are built on trust and honesty. This includes the most intimate relationships within families, and it also includes business and social relationships. Lying destroys the fabric of trust that makes such relationships possible. No wonder Paul wrote to Christians, "Wherefore putting away lying, speak every man truth with his neighbour: for we are members one of another" (Eph. 4:25).

Verse 28 also warns against flattery, which is one form of lying. The flatterer feeds the ego of someone else at the expense of the truth. Often the flatterer's motivation is to win the favor of the person being flattered because that person is able to give the flatterer something he wants.

Proverbs 6:16–20 lists seven things that the Lord hates. Three of these are sins of speech: "a lying tongue," "a false witness that speaketh lies," and "he that soweth discord among brethren."

2. Helpful speech (15:23; 16:24)

> **15:23 A man hath joy by the answer of his mouth: and a word spoken in due season, how good is it!**
>
> **16:24 Pleasant words are as an honeycomb, sweet to the soul, and health to the bones.**

The word translated "answer" means "apt answer" or "good answer." Thus, the idea in the first part of 15:23 is that joy results from speaking or hearing just the right answer. The last part of the same verse stresses well-timed speech. In other words, the person in Proverbs 15:23 says just the right thing at just the right time. The result is joy and good for all concerned.

Proverbs 16:23 compares pleasant words to the sweetness of honey. Such words bring happiness and health. We speak such words when we speak words of love, affirmation, comfort, and encouragement. When is the right time to speak such words? In recent years, the Lord has been trying to teach me that the best time to express love and appreciation is *today*.

3. Striking contrasts (15:1–2)

> **1 A soft answer turneth away wrath: but grievous words stir up anger.**
>
> **2 The tongue of the wise useth knowledge aright: but the mouth of fools poureth out foolishness.**

These two verses present two vivid contrasts between helpful and harmful speech. Verse 1 contrasts a soft answer with a grievous or harsh answer. The harsh words are those of a contentious person (26:21). They stir up and provoke anger. They fan the fires of misunderstanding. Soft words are quiet, thoughtful, and thus healing words. Such words have a calming effect. Potential strife is avoided. Peace becomes possible in actual strife. Jesus and Paul taught that believers should not retaliate by giving back evil for evil; instead we should give back good for evil (Matt. 5:38–48; Rom. 12:18–21).

AUGUST

16

1998

Verse 2 contrasts speech that imparts helpful knowledge with speech that is nothing more than foolishness. Speech is an amazing miracle. By making certain sounds, people can communicate their thoughts and knowledge to others. This miracle can be used to share what helps or what hurts, what enriches or what impoverishes, what enlightens or what confuses.

Parallelism in Hebrew Poetry

Parallelism is a device in which the second line of a couplet reinforces the first line by repetition (synonymous), contrast (antithetic), or elaboration (synthetic).

Synonymous parallelism:

Doth not wisdom cry?
and understanding put forth her voice?
Proverbs 8:1

Antithetic parallelism:

A soft answer turneth away wrath,
but grievous words stir up anger.
Proverbs 15:1

Synthetic parallelism:

Train up a child in the way he should go:
and when he is old, he will not depart from it.
Proverbs 22:6

APPLYING THE BIBLE

1. The power of words. Logan Smith is remembered for this line: "For the Pen is mightier than the Sword." The strange fact is that Smith heard a minister say that sentence and disagreed with it. What do you think?

2. War and words. Ralph Waldo Emerson wrote: "Eloquence a hundred times has turned the scale of war and peace at will." Can you recall instances where war (of one size or another) was averted by the use of conciliatory words? Can you think of when the reverse occurred, that is, when peace became war because of words?

3. A word fitly spoken. I once knew a pastor about whom I honestly thought, "He is the only person I know who can offend someone while trying to pay a compliment!" Perhaps that was too judgmental on my part, but it certainly made me pray that God would teach me how—and what—to speak. Remember the biblical statement about this: "A word fitly spoken is like apples of gold in pictures of silver" (Prov. 25:11). So, words are not only powerful; they can be beautiful too!

4. The power of words. Confucius said, "Without knowing the force of words, it is impossible to know men." Hitler manipulated people with words. His theory, which he often stated and boasted of, was to tell them a lie—the bigger the lie the better, because the bigger it was the more intensely they would believe it. Contrast this with the song that says of Jesus, "His lips with grace o'erflow."

5. Trusting Jesus. I once asked my mother about her favorite Bible verse. She quickly quoted the opening lines of John 14 where, among other things, Jesus said, "If it were not so, I would have told you." I asked her why she loved those words best. She said, "I don't know who to believe on earth, but I know I can believe Jesus because He said, 'If it were not so, I would have told you.'" She added, "Surely, He would not have lied to us." Surely! If truth is not important, why did Jesus say, "Ye shall know the truth, and the truth shall make you free" (John 8:32)?

6. Two proverbs.

- "Truth makes the devil blush." (Ask yourself: How is truth an enemy of the devil?)
- "Speak the truth and shame the devil." (Compare these two proverbs.)

7. The damage of lies. All lies will finally die. They have within themselves the seeds of their own destruction. Like fires, they finally burn themselves out. That is the good news, but the bad news is that they often burn up others before they burn out! Do you recall a lie someone told about you that was a terrible burden to bear? Do you remember words that you spoke that you wish you could retrieve?

8. Quick quotes.

- "When once a word is let loose in the earth, no power in earth or heaven can take it back!" (Anonymous).
- "A lie travels round the world while Truth is putting on her boots" (C. H. Spurgeon).
- "Words once spoken can never be recall'd" (Horace).
- "Thoughts unexpressed may sometimes fall back dead; but God himself can't kill them when they're said" (Will Carleton).
- "Four things come not back: the spoken word; the sped arrow; time past; and the neglected opportunity" (Omar Ibn Al-Halif).

TEACHING THE BIBLE

- *Main Idea:* We can choose to speak either helpful or harmful words.
- *Suggested Teaching Aim:* To lead adults to identify guidelines to help them watch what they say

A TEACHING OUTLINE

1. Use an illustration to introduce the Bible study.

2. Use five posters as silent teachers to enhance the Bible study.

3. Encourage members to develop guidelines to apply the Scriptures.

4. Use ranking to help members evaluate their own speech patterns.

Introduce the Bible Study

Use "The power of words" in "Applying the Bible" to introduce the Bible study. Suggest that words are indeed powerful, and we can hurt or help by what we say.

Search for Biblical Truth

IN ADVANCE, using the five "Quick quotes" in "Applying the Bible," make five large posters and place these around the room as silent teachers.

Write on a chalkboard or a large sheet of paper: *To help me watch what I say, I . . .* Distribute paper and pencils to members. Ask members silently to read Proverbs 12:18. Ask: Are there ever times when you should not tell the truth? Based on this verse, let the group finish the above sentence and write their guideline on the chalkboard. Ask them to copy it on their sheet of paper.

Ask members silently to read Proverbs 13:3; 21:23; 15:28; and 17:27. Ask: What situation did you encounter this past week when keeping your mouth shut was the wisest thing to do? Based on these verses, let the group finish the above sentence and write their guideline on the chalkboard. Ask them to copy it on their sheet of paper.

Ask members silently to read Proverbs 11:12–13. Read the following case study: Jim was a deacon and active in his church and community as a Christian businessman. He often spoke in churches for a layman's Bible group. He was well respected by all—except his wife and a few close friends; they knew how he belittled his wife every chance he had. Ask: Can a person be a "good" Christian and belittle others? Based on these verses, let the group finish the above sentence and write their guideline on the chalkboard. Ask them to copy it on their sheet of paper.

Ask members silently to read Proverbs 26:21, 28. Ask: Why do people flatter others? Based on these verses, let the group finish the above sentence and write their guideline on the chalkboard. Ask them to copy it on their sheet of paper.

Ask members silently to read Proverbs 15:23 and 16:24. Ask: Would you share with us when someone spoke the right word to you at the right time? Based on these verses, let the group finish the above sentence and write their guideline on the chalkboard. Ask them to copy it on their sheet of paper.

Ask members silently to read Proverbs 15:1–2. Ask: How can we make a practice of speaking gently? Based on these verses, let the group finish the above sentence and write their guideline on the chalkboard. Ask them to copy it on their sheet of paper.

Give the Truth a Personal Focus

Read the list of guidelines members have written. Ask members to look over the list of guidelines and silently rate themselves as to how well they fulfill these guidelines. Ask members to place their list where they can see it each morning and read it before they begin their daily activities.

Slow to Anger

AUGUST

23

1998

Basic Passages: Proverbs 12:16; 14:17, 29; 15:18; 16:32; 19:11; 22:24–25; 25:28; 27:4; 29:20, 22

Focal Passages: Proverbs 12:16; 14:17, 29; 15:18; 16:32; 19:11; 22:24–25; 25:28; 27:4; 29:20, 22

The Letter of James has much in common with the Wisdom Writings of the Old Testament. "Wisdom" is stressed (1:5; 3:13–18), and James dealt with some of the same practical areas of everyday living found in the Book of Proverbs. He had a lot to say about sins of the tongue (3:1–12). In James 1:19, he mentioned speech in connection with anger, "Let every man be swift to hear, slow to speak, slow to wrath." Many scattered verses in Proverbs deal with the importance of being slow to anger.

Study Aim: *To identify differences between angry people and people who are slow to anger*

STUDYING THE BIBLE

OUTLINE AND SUMMARY

I. Expressing or Restraining Anger? (Prov. 14:29; 29:20)

II. Troublemakers or Peacemakers? (Prov. 15:18; 29:22)

III. Out-of-Control or Self-Control? (Prov. 16:32; 25:28)

IV. Enemies or Friends? (Prov. 22:24–25)

V. Retaliation or Forgiveness? (Prov. 12:16; 14:17; 19:11; 27:4)

1. Worse than quick-tempered (14:17; 27:4)

2. Practicing forgiveness (12:16; 19:11)

An angry person is quick to express anger in word and deed, but a wise person is slow to anger (14:29; 29:20). Angry people stir up strife, but people who are slow to anger make peace (15:18; 29:22). Angry people are walking time bombs, but people who are slow to anger show self-control and inner strength (16:32; 25:28). People are warned not to make friends with angry people lest they be influenced to become like their friends (22:24–25). Jealousy or plotting revenge can be worse than being quick-tempered (14:17: 27:4). Practicing forgiveness requires bearing the hurt and setting it aside as a barrier to future relationships (12:16; 19:11).

I. Expressing or Restraining Anger? (Prov. 14:29; 29:20)

14:29 He that is slow to wrath is of great understanding: but he that is hasty of spirit exalteth folly.

29:20 Seest thou a man that is hasty in his words? there is more hope of a fool than of him.

"Hasty of spirit" in Proverbs 14:29 is contrasted with being "slow to wrath." Therefore, the hasty spirit likely referred to being quick to feel and express anger. People who are slow to anger are people of good sense and understanding; whereas, people who quickly lose their tempers exemplify and exalt folly.

Proverbs 29:20 says nothing specific about people of bad temper, but the verse does warn against one being "hasty in his words." And as we saw in the session for August 16, Proverbs often linked loss of temper with hasty words (15:1; 26:21). The wise writer of Proverbs held out more hope for fools than for people who speak before they think. More often than not, hasty words are spoken in the heat of great emotion and cause harm to all concerned.

Everyone gets angry at times. The question is: How should people deal in the most healthy way with their anger? Some people argue that we should immediately express our anger, but unrestrained expressions of anger are often destructive. Jesus warned against the kind of anger that expresses itself in name-calling (Matt. 5:22). Paul warned against holding a grudge (Eph. 4:26–27). He wrote, "Let all bitterness, and wrath, and anger, and clamour, and evil speaking, be put away from you, with all malice" (Eph. 4:31).

This does not mean that we should simply bottle up our anger within us or try to deny that we ever get angry. Wise marriage counselors advise postponing discussing conflicts until tempers have cooled; then follow certain ground rules about how to deal with angry feelings in healthy, helpful ways.

II. Troublemakers or Peacemakers? (Prov. 15:18; 29:22)

15:18 A wrathful man stirreth up strife: but he that is slow to anger appeaseth strife.

29:22 An angry man stirreth up strife, and a furious man aboundeth in transgression.

The word translated "appeaseth" in Proverbs 15:18 can be translated "quiets" or "pacifies." People who express their anger freely stir up strife. By contrast, people who are slow to anger have a calming influence. This verse is similar to the contrast between the effect of harsh words and soft words in Proverbs 15:1. Angry people use harsh words to attack others and thus to start arguments; then they keep stirring up strife with their angry words. Proverbs 29:22 makes clear that angry people who stir up strife are sinning and leading others into situations in which they will commit sin. This is the force of the word "aboundeth."

Rather than allowing our anger to make us troublemakers, people of faith and love are called to be peacemakers. Jesus said that peacemakers are blessed because they are recognized as children of the God of peace (Matt. 5:9). By exercising restraint on our own anger, we can have a calming effect on strife—whether potential or actual.

III. Out-of-Control or Self-Control? (Prov. 16:32; 25:28)

16:32 He that is slow to anger is better than the mighty; and he that ruleth his spirit than he that taketh a city.

25:28 He that hath no rule over his own spirit is like a city that is broken down, and without walls.

These two verses use vivid images to contrast people with self-control and people who are out-of-control. The person with self-control is compared to a mighty warrior who is able to rule an entire city. The person without self-control is compared to a city with broken-down walls. In ancient times, each city had walls as a defense against enemies and wild animals. Thus a city with broken walls was helpless and vulnerable to enemy attack.

We live in a society of people who are living on the edge. They are ready to explode in anger at the slightest provocation. They and those around them are as vulnerable as an ancient city without walls. Abuse and even murder happen every day because people's emotions are out-of-control.

By contrast, maintaining self-control in a violent society requires great inner strength. People who have conquered their own emotions are confident people of great strength. People of faith, of course, know that self-control comes from a right relation with God. Paul wrote, "I can do all things through Christ which strengtheneth me" (Phil. 4:13). He would never have claimed to be able to do all things in his own strength.

IV. Enemies or Friends? (Prov. 22:24–25)

24 Make no friendship with an angry man; and with a furious man thou shalt not go:

25 Lest thou learn his ways, and get a snare to thy soul.

As we have noted, much of Proverbs is in the form of teachings of a wise father to his son. We have also noted that the father warned his son against associating with evil people. Proverbs 22:24–25 contains a warning against making friends with angry people like those described elsewhere in Proverbs. Parents in every generation can identify with the concern of the father who wrote these words. As children grow up, friends become increasingly important to them. During adolescence, many youth are strongly influenced by their friends. If they have chosen the wrong kind of friends, they will be under pressure to do things that are contrary to what their parents have taught them is right.

This is not a modern phenomenon, nor is it confined to youth. All of us are influenced by our friends and associates. Even people of spiritual strength are not immune from the temptations that come from such associations. In Galatians 6:1, Paul gave instructions about seeking to restore a fellow Christian who has fallen into sin. Part of the verse includes a warning to the would-be rescuer lest the rescuer also become involved in the same sin.

Proverbs 22:24–25 warns against making friends with people who are angry and quick-tempered. Many a Christian has married an angry person expecting to reform him or her—only to become the victim of either verbal or physical abuse. Association with angry people makes us potential victims, and it tends to influence us to adopt the same destructive emotions and patterns of behavior.

V. Retaliation or Forgiveness? (Prov. 12:16; 14:17; 19:11; 27:4)

1. Worse than quick-tempered (14:17; 27:4)

27:4 Wrath is cruel, and anger is outrageous; but who is able to stand before envy?

14:17 He that is soon angry dealeth foolishly: and a man of wicked devices is hated.

The meaning of these verses is not obvious on the surface. The word translated "envy" in Proverbs 27:4 is better translated "jealousy." The same word is found in Proverbs 6:34 and in Song of Solomon 8:6, where it refers to the jealousy of a husband. "For jealousy is the rage of a man: therefore he will not spare in the day of vengeance" (Prov. 6:34). This warning is in a passage that tells a son the dangers of committing adultery. One danger is the terrible vengeance that the jealous husband will inflict.

Thus, the point of 27:4 is that in some ways jealousy is even worse than wrath and anger. These are described in strong terms as "cruel" and "outrageous," but the writer asks who will be able to withstand the rage of a jealous husband. This rage may be expressed immediately, or it may fester until a future day of vengeance.

Proverbs 14:17 also requires some clarification. Some translations follow one version of the ancient text, and some follow another. Some, for example, see the verse as a contrast between a foolish man who gets angry and a prudent man who shows patience. The Hebrew text, however, sees the second clause as contrasting two forms of anger, not anger and patience. The "man of wicked devices" is a person who plots intrigue against his enemies. The first clause describes the quick-tempered person who immediately blows up with anger. The second clause describes the person who nurses his grudge and lays a long-range plot to get even with those who have slighted him. Both kinds of anger are dangerous and destructive; but in many ways, the second is worse. The first person may commit a crime of passion in the heat of the moment, but the second person acts coldly with premeditation.

2. Practicing forgiveness (12:16; 19:11)

12:16 A fool's wrath is presently known: but a prudent man covereth shame.

19:11 The discretion of a man deferreth his anger; and it is his glory to pass over a transgression.

These two verses also require some explanation. The word translated "presently" in 12:16 does not mean at some time in the future; it means right away. The word translated "covereth" can mean to conceal or to hide, but it can also be used to mean "forgive." David used the word that way in Psalm 32:1, "Blessed is he whose transgression is forgiven, whose sin is covered" (see also Ps. 85:2; Neh. 4:5). "Shame" referred to something done to insult or hurt the prudent man. He had two choices:

he could strike back like the fool in the first clause of the verse, or he could forgive the insult by acting as if it had not happened.

Proverbs 19:11 uses "deferred" not to mean postponed with plans to retaliate later, like the wicked person of Proverbs 14:17. The word was used to describe someone who is patient and forbearing, slow to anger. A person shows discretion by being slow to anger, but he shows his true glory by actually passing over the transgression against him. The word translated "pass over" is used in Micah 7:18 to mean the same thing as "pardon."

These two verses illustrate two characteristics of forgiveness. Covering sin refers to the process of bearing the pain that is necessary to forgive. The cross reminds us that forgiveness is possible when the injured party is willing to absorb the hurt without striking back. Passing over sin refers to forgiving and forgetting. That is, the one who forgives sets aside the hurt as if it had not happened. The past sin is not dredged back up from time to time. It is covered and passed over forever.

APPLYING THE BIBLE

1. Anger and the soul. "In his 'Ethics,' (IV,5,7) Aristotle long ago declared that men are angry for the wrong reasons, with the wrong people, in a wrong way, for too long a time. Even if such exhibitions of ungodly anger did not dishonor God, and work havoc in the hearts of people nearby, such lack of Christian self—control would do untold harm to one's own soul."[1]

2. Anger and the body. E. Stanley Jones once said, "The British Medical Association says that 'there is not a single cell of the body totally removed from the influence of mind and emotion.' So the attitudes of mind and emotion do not stay attitudes; they pass over into definite physical effects."[2]

3. Headaches. I heard a taped message by a Christian medical doctor who said, "Ninety-seven percent of all migraines are due to problems with other people—repressed anger, etc., in interpersonal relationships." The speaker went on to say that he had done a wide survey of various clinics dealing with migraines and found that, among about 20,000 sufferers, "nineteen out of twenty hold grudges." He added that it was very rare for these types not to be helped immediately by counsel related to handling repressed anger and getting things right with others. (My personal view is that while emotions do certainly strongly affect our bodies, it is certainly possible for genetics to play a strong role in migraines.)

4. Professional hater? I received a letter from a viewer of one of our televised services who wrote about her husband's hate. She said "I never learned to hate, but my husband is a professional at it." She went on to tell how his hatred had disturbed their family. I've met all kinds of professionals, but never a professional hater! Imagine an "All-American Hate Team," or a "Hater's Hall of Fame," or "The Annual Haters All-Star Game!" Would you make the team?

5. Hostile heart or trusting heart? Syndicated columnist George Will wrote an article entitled, "Anger—The Deadliest Sin." Citing the writings of Dr. Redford Williams of Duke University, Will reports that "hostility is hard on the heart." He explains, "New learning about the physiology of stress (brain activities stimulated, bodily chemicals released) points Williams to old religious teachings about living. Be more tranquil, less worldly. 'If yours is a hostile heart, you need to change it into a more trusting heart.'"

6. Hatred among Christians. Followers of Christ are sometimes, strangely, very capable of precisely the same anger/hate seen in non-Christians. In his poem "Locksley Hall Sixty Years Later," Alfred Lord Tennyson wrote:

> Love your enemy, bless your haters,
> said the greatest of the great;
> Christian love among the Churches
> looked the twin of heathen hate.

7. Never satisfied. Sometimes people have made up their minds to be angry, no matter what the situation. A man came home after working the night and demanded that his dutiful wife prepare two eggs for his breakfast, one fried and the other scrambled. When she brought a beautiful breakfast to the table, he banged his fist on the table and said, "There you go; you've done it again; you've fried the wrong egg!"

TEACHING THE BIBLE

- *Main Idea:* Those who control their anger are wise.
- *Suggested Teaching Aim:* To lead adults to identify ways to control their anger

A TEACHING OUTLINE

1. Use an illustration to introduce the Bible study.

2. Use strip posters and a chart to guide the search for biblical truth.

3. Use lecture and group discussion to explain the Scripture.

4. Use a visual to give the truth a personal focus.

Introduce the Bible Study

Use "Professional hater" in "Applying the Bible" to introduce the Bible study.

Search for Biblical Truth

IN ADVANCE, make five strip posters with the following questions about anger:

- Should you express or restrain anger?
- Are you a troublemaker or a peacemaker?
- Are you out-of-control, or do you exercise self-control?
- Does it do any harm to be friends with angry people?
- Do you practice retaliation or forgiveness?

On a chalkboard or a large sheet of paper write:

How to Control Your Temper

Don't	Do

Place the first question on the wall and ask members to respond. Ask a member to read Proverbs 14:29; 29:20. Lecture briefly using "Studying the Bible" to explain: (1) "hasty of spirit"; (2) Jesus (Matt. 5:22) and Paul (Eph. 4:26—27) warned against unrestrained expressions of anger. Ask members to write on the chart a negative (Don't speak before you think.) and a positive (Be patient.) statement based on these verses. Members' responses may differ and still be correct.

DISCUSS: Why should we not simply bottle up our anger within us or try to deny that we ever get angry?

Place the second question on the wall and ask members to respond. Ask a member to read Proverbs 15:18; 29:22. Lecture briefly using "Studying the Bible" to explain: (1) People who express their anger freely stir up strife; (2) Rather than allowing our anger to make us troublemakers, people of faith and love are called to be peacemakers. Ask members to write on the chart a negative (Don't stir up strife.) and a positive (Be a peacemaker.) statement based on these verses.

DISCUSS: How can we be angry and not sin as Ephesians 4:26 suggests?

Place the third question on the wall and ask members to respond. Ask a member to read Proverbs 16:32; 25:28. Lecture briefly using "Studying the Bible" to explain: (1) two vivid images contrasting people with self-control and people who are out-of-control; (2) maintaining self-control in a violent society requires great inner strength; (3) and this inner strength comes from Christ. Ask members to write on the chart a negative (Don't lose self-control.) and a positive (Control your anger.) statement based on these verses.

DISCUSS: What can you do to claim Christ's power to strengthen your self-control?

Place the fourth question on the wall and ask members to respond. Ask a member to read Proverbs 22:24—25. Lecture briefly using "Studying the Bible" to explain: (1) the importance of children and adults choosing the right kinds of friends; (2) and when adults choose the wrong kind of partner, serious trouble can result. Ask members to write on the chart a negative (Don't hang around angry people.) and a positive (Associate with peacemakers.) statement based on these verses.

DISCUSS: How can we avoid being hurt by others' anger?

Place the fifth question on the wall and ask members to respond. Ask a member to read 14:17; 27:4. Lecture briefly using "Studying the Bible" to explain: (1) the meaning of the word translated "envy"; (2) and the two possible understandings of 14:17. Ask members to write on the chart a negative (Don't fly off the handle.) and a positive (Forgive.) statement based on these verses.

DISCUSS: How can we "forgive and forget" when someone has wronged us?

AUGUST

23

1998

Give the Truth a Personal Focus

Ask members to examine the list of do's and don'ts they have compiled. Let them add any other statements they have found effective. Say: Today we have talked about how to control our anger. Here are five steps that will help:

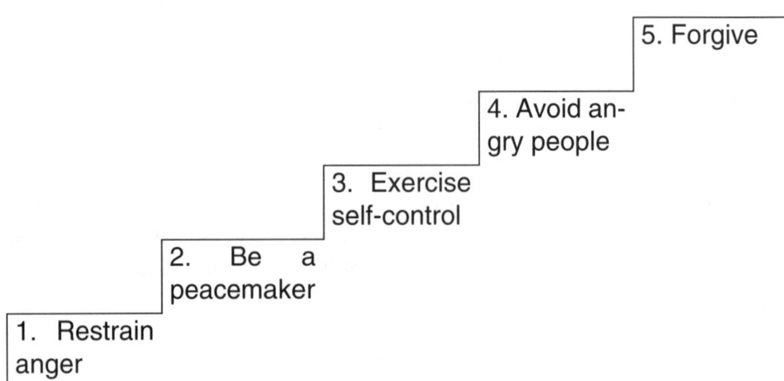

Close with prayer that members will make progress in controlling their anger this week.

---

1. Andrew Blackwood, *The Growing Minister* (Nashville: Abingdon Press, 1960), 109.
2. E. Stanley Jones, *Growing Spiritually* (Nashville: Abingdon, 1953), 228.

Wisdom for Family Relationships

AUGUST

30

1998

Basic Passages: Proverbs 4:1–5; 6:20; 10:1; 22:6; 31:26–28

Focal Passages: Proverbs 4:1–5; 6:20; 10:1; 22:6; 31:26–28

Family is another area where practical wisdom is needed for everyday life. The Book of Proverbs, therefore, has many passages about family relationships. Special emphasis is given to what parents teach in the home to their children and to the responses that children make to this teaching.

Study Aim: *To explain the importance of proper teaching of children by their parents*

STUDYING THE BIBLE

OUTLINE AND SUMMARY

I. Teaching and Learning in the Home (Prov. 4:1–5; 6:20)
1. Responsibility of parents as teachers (4:1–4)
2. Responsibility of children as learners (4:5; 6:20)

II. Joy and Anguish of Parenting (Prov. 10:1; 22:6)
1. Gladness or grief (10:1)
2. Lasting effect of childhood training (22:6)

III. Godly Wife and Mother (Prov. 31:26–28)
1. Teacher and homemaker (31:26–27)
2. Honored by her husband and children (31:28)

Each generation of parents is responsible for teaching faith and godly living to their children (4:1–4). Children are responsible for learning and obeying what they are taught (4:5; 6:20). Parents of a wise son have joy; parents of a foolish son have anguish (10:1). Proper training of children by parents has a lasting effect (22:6). A godly mother is both teacher and homemaker (31:26–27). Her children and husband express love and appreciation for her (31:28).

I. Teaching and Learning in the Home (Prov. 4:1–5; 6:20)

1. Responsibility of parents as teachers (4:1–4)

1 Hear, ye children, the instruction of a father, and attend to know understanding.

2 For I give you good doctrine, forsake ye not my law.

3 For I was my father's son, tender and only beloved in the sight of my mother.

4 He taught me also, and said unto me, Let thine heart retain my words: keep my commandments, and live.

Throughout our study of Proverbs, we have noted that the basic setting was a father teaching his son. Many scholars claim that this fatherly wisdom later was used by teachers in schools. This passage, however, clearly shows that the home was the original setting for teaching. The father in verse 1 describes in verse 3 how his own father had taught him. Although fathers were the primary teachers, mothers also were involved (1:8; 6:20; 10:1; 31:26). The word "children" in verse 1 is actually "sons." In that day, daughters were not given the same kind of instruction as the sons. However, the principles in Proverbs apply also to girls.

The word translated "doctrine" in verse 2 means "what is received." The stress is on the instruction to be received by each new generation of children and youth. For the Hebrews, this included not only instructions about faith but also teachings about how to live. Deuteronomy 6:4–9 includes both. Proverbs 1:7 says that the beginning of wisdom is the fear of the Lord, but much of the book's content deals with how to live.

The father's long-range objective for home training was that his sons might "live." The wise father knew from Deuteronomy 30 and from experience that faith and obedience are the way to life as God intended. Disobedience leads to death.

Notice the emphasis on each generation teaching the next generation. As someone has said, "Each generation is only one generation away from paganism." Grandchildren as well as children were to be taught (Deut. 6:2).

2. Responsibility of children as learners (4:5; 6:20)

> **4:5 Get wisdom, get understanding: forget it not; neither decline from the words of my mouth.**
>
> **6:20 My son, keep thy father's commandment, and forsake not the law of thy mother.**

These two verses stress the responsibility of children to respond positively to what they are taught by their parents. (Notice that both father and mother are mentioned.) Review the words in verses 1–4 that challenge children: "hear," "attend," "forsake ye not," "retain," and "keep." Proverbs 4:5 adds, "get," "forget it not," "neither decline." Proverbs 6:20 repeats "keep" and "forsake not." The word translated "decline" means "stretch down or out." It is used here to mean "turn away from." The word "get" is repeated for emphasis. The word means to acquire or bring into your own possession; and it probably implies getting it at any price, so great is its value.

Parents must do their best to teach and impart wisdom to their children, but the children must respond. Can a parent give a child a college education? A parent can help to make such an education possible, but only the young person can choose to do what is needed to take advantage of the opportunity to learn. Parents can do their best to teach and influence their children in the right way; but they cannot force, control, or program their children to be what they want them to be.

II. Joy and Anguish of Parenting (Prov. 10:1; 22:6)

1. Gladness or grief (10:1)

1 The proverbs of Solomon. A wise son maketh a glad father: but a foolish son is the heaviness of his mother.

Proverbs 1:1 introduces the book, "The proverbs of Solomon the son of David, king of Israel." Solomon was noted for his wisdom in general and for his proverbs in particular (1 Kings 4:32). Proverbs 25:1 introduces a later section, "These are also proverbs of Solomon, which the men of Hezekiah king of Judah copied out." Two other writers are mentioned: Agur (AY gur, 30:1) and Lemuel (LEM yoo uhl, 31:1).

Some Bible students believe that Solomon wrote all the proverbs in the book except for chapters 30–31. Others believe that Solomon was the source of much of the book but that he also compiled other proverbs into a form for sharing. For example, he may have included traditional proverbs that parents had used to teach their young.

At any rate, the mention again of Solomon in 10:1 after the earlier introduction in 1:1 divides the discourse section of Proverbs 1–9 from the shorter proverbs that begin in 10:1.

The word translated "heaviness" means "sorrow" or "grief." Hebrew poetry uses parallel expressions at times, and at other times it used contrasting expressions. The contrast is between the wise and the foolish son. The father and the mother are not intended to be contrasts but partners in the joy and anguish of parents. The point is that a wise son is a joy to both parents, and a foolish son causes grief for both.

As every parent knows, being a parent is risky. Parenting is a mixture of joy and anguish. Listen to the anguish in David's cry after he learned of the death of his rebellious son Absalom (AB suh luhm, 2 Sam. 18:33). By contrast, Timothy was a joy to his mother, grandmother, and surrogate father Paul (2 Tim. 1:1–5).

2. Lasting effect of childhood training (22:6)

6 Train up a child in the way he should go: and when he is old, he will not depart from it.

Proverbs 22:6 is one of the most famous verses in the book. The verse underscores the importance of what children are taught when they are young. The words translated "in the way he should go" mean literally "according to his way." These words have been interpreted in at least three ways: (1) the words may mean that each child is to be trained in a way personally suited for that individual child; (2) the words may mean that each child is be trained in a way best suited for children in general; or (3) the more traditional interpretation does not stress how the training is done so much as what is taught. According to this popular view, parents are to do what Paul wrote in Ephesians 6:4: "Bring them up in the nurture and admonition of the Lord."

Each interpretation contains wise guidance for parents. Christian parents are concerned to teach their children to trust the Lord and to live according to His Word. At the same time, wise parents will remember that people at different ages learn best if the approaches are suited to their age level. Children are not adults. Wise parents will also recognize that each of their children is an individual who can best be reached in certain ways.

The larger question about Proverbs 22:6 concerns the meaning of the last part. Is this intended to be an unconditional promise? That is, does God's Word guarantee that each child who is properly taught at home will eventually turn out all right? Not everyone will give the same answer. Personally, I believe we must keep two things in mind about this promise. For one thing, the Bible, the Book of Proverbs, and life itself show that some children of godly parents choose to go the wrong way. Absalom did. The words that challenge children to hear and not forget in Proverbs 4:1–5 and 6:20 show that the children must make their own choices.

The other factor is that no parents are perfect, and no childhood training is perfect. David's grief was partly due to feelings of guilt. However, even people who are better examples and teachers to their children sometimes experience the anguish of a rebellious son or daughter.

What promise then can parents claim from Proverbs 22:6? They can take comfort in the fact that they have done their best to impart the way of faith and righteousness to their children. This gives the children a strong influence toward what is right, and it surely offers them a choice. Contrast children who received a Christian education in the home with children who received no such training. The latter group is subject only to the evil influences of childhood, youth, and adult life. In essence, by withholding a Christian education, their parents have robbed them of an opportunity to choose the Christian way of life.

III. Godly Wife and Mother (Prov. 31:26–28)

1. Teacher and homemaker (31:26–27)

26 She openeth her mouth with wisdom; and in her tongue is the law of kindness.

27 She looketh well to the ways of her household, and eateth not the bread of idleness.

Proverbs 31:10–31 is a tribute to a godly wife and mother. Verse 26 stresses her teaching role, which is by example as well as by precept. She teaches wisdom with kindness. The word translated "kindness" is the Old Testament word expressing the covenant love of God for His people and the type of kindness that godly people are to show toward one another. (See comments on "mercy" in Prov. 3:3 in the session for July 12.) The word carries the ideas of kindness and loyalty. A godly mother is surely both.

Verse 27 stresses her role as homemaker. This verse summarizes the description of her diligence in verses 13–19. She is far from idle. This is similar to the English proverb, "Man may work from sun to sun, but a woman's work is never done." Within recent years, the role of homemaker has received a lot of bad press. According to the Bible, nothing is more demanding or rewarding than being the kind of wife and mother described in Proverbs 31:10–31.

2. Honored by her husband and children (31:28)

28 Her children arise up, and call her blessed; her husband also, and he praiseth her.

Verse 28 gives one important factor in finding fulfillment and joy as a homemaker. In a godly home, the husband expresses his love and appreciation to his wife and to others about her. Likewise, when the children are mature enough to appreciate what she has done, they express their love and appreciation for her. Proverbs 31:28 provides an example of the "pleasant" words described in Proverbs 16:24 as sweet and healing (see session for Aug. 16).

Nothing is more important in human relationships than expressing love and appreciation. This is especially true of the most intimate and personal relationships of the family. Husbands and wives can enrich or impoverish their relationship, depending on whether they often express love and appreciation for each other; and nothing so brightens a child as a parent's genuine approval and love. Likewise, amid all the joys and anguishes of parenting, nothing is so satisfying to parents as for their children to speak and to show that they love and appreciate their parents.

"She layeth her hand to the spindle" (Prov. 31:19). (Source: Holman Pictorial Collection of Biblical Antiquities, Holman Bible Publishers, Nashville, TN [The Louvre, Paris]).

APPLYING THE BIBLE

1. Parents teaching children. Our study today focuses on parents' teaching their children. The Bible, from one cover to the other, makes that emphasis, a much-needed emphasis in a culture which so readily gives up the education of its children to the state and to the church.

2. Battle for the mind. A book appeared some years ago entitled *The Battle for the Mind.* That's the story of our civilization. That's the story of every civilization!

3. The importance of the family. In his book *Christianity and World Issues,* T. B. Maston wrote, "The family is . . . a more important educational institution than the school. . . . a more important institution for law and order than the state . . . [and] a more basically determinative religious institution than the church."

4. Heredity and environment. The two most determinative factors in our lives—genetics and environment (or, "nature and nurture")—are largely determined by parents. We parents can do little with the "nature" part, but we must do all we can about the "nurture" part.

5. Breaking the cycle. What advice would you give to young parents who say they were brought up in "dysfunctional" homes. They explain, "We just can't break the negative cycle." What place does the church play in this matter?

6. Education of the heart. In his book *The Closing of the American Heart,* Ronald H. Nash writes, "The inadequacies of contemporary education are not exclusively matters of the mind. Traditional religious and moral values are under assault at every level of public and higher education. . . . Our educational crisis is to some extent a closing of the American mind. But it is also something more profound, a closing of the American *heart*." The home, aided by the church, is the best context for the education of the heart of a child.

7. Parenting today. Politician-preacher Jesse Jackson said, "All parents are parenting against today's culture."[1] List several key values of your culture—values your children are learning—and contrast them with those of the Bible.

8. Misinformation. Humorist Josh Billings once said, "It is better not to know so much than to know so many things that ain't so." What an apt description of people who "know" many things but do not know God!

9. Teaching by example. I love the story about the man who was demanding educational discipline in his boy. The man shouted to his son, "Do you know what Abraham Lincoln was doing when he was your age?" The boy said, "No, but I know what he was doing when he was your age—he was the president of the country!"

10. He quit! A man told his son, "You have to persevere. Remember Robert Fulton. And Abraham Lincoln. And George Washington Carver. And Irving McPringle." The boy asked, quizzically, "Who on earth was Irving McPringle?" The dad answered, "See; nobody knows him; he quit!"

11. Successful failures. *Fortune,* a leading business magazine, reports, "For all their brains and competence, powerful, successful executives and professionals often have more trouble raising kids than all but the very poor. Alas, the intensity and single-mindedness that make for corporate achievement are often the opposite of the qualities needed to be an effective parent." One young man, reared in such a setting, said, "With my dad, all I got was a ten-year busy signal."[2]

TEACHING THE BIBLE

➧ *Main Idea:* God's Word contains instructions to fathers, mothers, and children about how they are to relate.

Suggested Teaching Aim: To lead adults to examine some of the Bible's teachings about their responsibilities in raising children

A TEACHING OUTLINE

1. Use recall to introduce the Bible study.
2. Use a chart and two posters to guide the search for biblical truth.
3. Use a listening assignment to involve members.
4. Use lecture and discussion to explain the biblical truth.
5. Use personal examination to give the truth a personal focus.

Introduce the Bible Study

Ask: What lessons do you remember your parents teaching you? How did they do this? What effect did it have on your life? Allow several members to respond.

Search for Biblical Truth

IN ADVANCE, write on a chalkboard or a large sheet of paper the bold headings (members will add italicized phrases):

What Makes a Christian Home?
Role of Fathers

1. *Give good advice (4:2)*
2. *Teach children correctly (22:6)*
3. *Express love and appreciation to the mother (31:28)*

Role of Mothers

1. *Teach children correctly (22:6)*
2. *Teach wisdom (31:26)*
3. *Care for her household (31:27)*
4. *Work hard (31:27)*

Role of Children

1. *Do right as adults (22:6)*
2. *Express love and appreciation to mother (31:28)*
3. *Make parents proud instead of sad (10:1)*
4. *Obey parents' teaching (4:5; 6:20)*

IN ADVANCE, make two posters and place them on the wall: "Each generation is only one generation away from paganism"; and "Train up a child in the way he should go: and when he is old, he will not depart from it" (Prov. 22:6).

Ask a third of the class to listen for responsibilities the father has in a Christian home; a third to listen for the mother's responsibilities; and a third to listen for the children's responsibilities.

Ask a member to read 4:1–4. Point out that what the Bible says about fathers also applies to mothers; what the Bible says about sons also applies to daughters. Ask: Where does this teaching take place? (In the home.) Why can we not delegate spiritual and moral instructions to the state and to the church? Why would the instruction in 4:4 ("Keep my commandments, and live.") still be good advice? Call members' attention to the poster: "Each generation is only one generation away from paganism." Ask if they agree and why. Ask members to suggest responsibilities for the chart. The italicized phrases are suggestions only; list all ideas members suggest that are biblically based.

Ask a member to read 4:5 and 6:20 and ask members to suggest responsibilities for the chart.

Ask a member to read 10:1 and 22:6. Point out the poster of 22:6. Using "Studying the Bible," share three possible meanings of 22:6. Ask members which interpretation they prefer. Ask: Does the promise in 22:6 guarantee that each child who is properly taught at home will turn out right? What promises can parents claim from 22:6? Ask members to suggest responsibilities for the chart.

Ask a member to read 31:26–28. Ask: What two characteristics does a godly mother exhibit? (Wisdom and kindness.) According to 31:28, what responsibilities do children and husbands have in their relationship to their mother and wife? (To express love and appreciation.) Ask members to suggest responsibilities for the chart.

Give the Truth a Personal Focus

Ask members to look at the list on the chart. Ask: How, at the stage of life you are in, do these statements affect you? (If you teach a class where members do not have children at home, lead them to see that they can help encourage these roles in families with children.) Close with a prayer for all families that they may have a Christian home.

---

1. Jesse Jackson, *St. Petersburg Times,* 16 December 1993: 22A.
2. "Why Grade 'A' Execs Get an 'F' as Parents," *Fortune* (1 January 1990).